Behold the Hand of God

The Right hand of fellowship

in a Left Handed world

Kingdom Alignment brings us into Kingdom Dimension

Dr. Kenneth DeWayne Grimble

Cover design concept drawing by Sarah Newton
Graphic Design of Book Cover by Ricky Saratt

Kingdom Empowerment Network Group
Publisher:
P.O. Box 3002 Springfield, IL 62708
Library of Congress Control Number: TXu 1-793-438

ISBN-13: 978-0981976976
ISBN-10: 0981976972

For Worldwide Distribution
Printed in the U.S.A

ACKNOWLEDGEMENTS

Behold the hand of God is a brilliant God-inspired kingdom building revelation! This book is applicable now within the body of Christ, in our left handed world. The vision is clear, alignment between the body of Christ and God's intended purpose for the church will lead us into kingdom dimension. This book is a must read for every believer and any level of spiritual maturity to gain the right perspective on church purpose and church leadership.

Katherine Jones, Senior Elder of Ramah Temple of Deliverance, San Diego California.

"*He* that *hath* an *ear, let him hear* what the Spirit saith unto the Churches; Nevertheless I have *somewhat* against thee, because thou hast left thy first love." - (Revelation 2:4,7) *"Behold the hand of God: The Right hand of fellowship in a left handed world."*, is a must read book to the modern day Church. Apostle Kenneth D. Grimble has conveyed the very heartbeat of God in this writing. Too often, the traditions of men, self-promotion, pride, and the desire to be a part of the "old boys club", have blinded clergymen, as well as laypersons from God's perfect order causing them to err. This writing exemplifies the prophetic "falling away of the Church" due to apostasy; as the sudden return of Jesus Christ is near. We should not be surprised, for "it is written". In (2 Thessalonians 2:3) we are told "Let no man deceive you by any means; for that day shall come, except there come a falling away first, and that man of sin be revealed, the son of perdition".

Paula A. Sanford, Senior Elder of Paula Sanford Ministries, Inc, Galesburg, Illinois

In the past several years, the Lord has been speaking to His Leaders, His Son's and Daughter's concerning "Spiritual Alignment". Many have acknowledge the call of God over our lives, while others have merely called themselves into the official office of the five fold ministry and administrative offices with the blessings of the Lord. This book is very revelatory and has placed a fire in my belly as an Apostle and a spiritual Mother responsible for many Son's and Daughter's, to help nurture in love and bring correction to them in a better way that they obey the voice of God in their perspective Offices. Those who have been improperly covered can fall into pitfalls, snares and the subtle traps of the devil, while they occupy their office of ministry which can cause them away from the faith, destroy the lives of others and invoke the wrath of God on their life. 2 Peter 1:10 says, "Wherefore the rather, brethren, given diligence to make your calling and election sure: for if ye do these things, ye shall never fall:" You must know who it is that has called you to this ministry, before you can function gracefully with the anointing in order to impact Heaven and become an asset to the Body of Christ. In today's society this book is very spontaneous and timely to help bring guidance, correction, instruction, understanding, and yes Rebuke to Leaders in the Church across the board. I encourage the reader to seek the heart of God as you hear what the Spirit of the Lord is saying for the Church and its Leaders.

No longer shall we settle for another level in our perspective Offices, gifting and calling. This book will cause you to cry out for more of God and the dimensions of His order and anointing.

Apostle Robin Blue
Robin Blue Ministries, Inc Phoenix, AZ

"Behold the Hand of God, The Right Hand of Fellowship in the Left Handed World" is bound to be a blessing and Rhema for the body of Christ. It contains truth of the present day church, and revelation of the fellowship that Adam lost in the garden. He also give us an insight of true relationship and right fellowship. I fully endorse this project as this book will prove to guide us to our God given density.

Apostle Anthony Burns
Presiding Prelate & Chief Apostle of Anointed Word Kingdom Assembly, Orlando, FL

"Behold the Hand of God: The Right Hand of fellowship In a left Handed World" should be required reading for every Five Fold leader to apply to their leadership. Apostle Kenneth D. Grimble has profoundly gazed the face of God. The principles, truths, and life applications are biblically driven. I have the same congenial love for my spiritual Father's Mandate for kingdom alignment, which is important for spiritual sons to have. This book should be "Obligatory" reading for all, Church leaders as well. I consider this book a valuable tool for leaders, in order to bring a revival of Kingdom alignment back to God's church and throughout the Nations of the World.

Prophet Curtis L. Marsh
Suffragan Bishop, and Founder, Cathedral Kingdom of Worship Empowerment Center Lillington, NC

"Behold the Hand of God: The Right Hand of Fellowship In a left Handed World is an instrument for Five Fold Leaders & Bishops.   This book is geared towards those who are ministering the word of God in this end time season. One of the greatest defaults in ministries, churches and fellowships is when one does not recognize their designated office and its need to correct displacement. For it is one thing to know your calling but another to serve in its proper place of alignment. This book will serve as a catalyst for those who are hungry to know their role in the body of Christ.   I have found this book to be inspirational and educational.

Howard L. Collier Presiding Bishop of New Life International Covenant Fellowship Inc., Springfield, IL

ENDORSEMENTS

Behold the Hand of God, The Right Hand of Fellowship In a Left Handed World is a book of encouragement and enlightenment to the body of Christ. This book is perceived to bare precious seed and fruit worldwide and in the market place. To all that will join me and applaud you as one of the most dynamic and prolific orators, your writing has the flair and ability to touch the hearts of leaders, administrators, mentors and all of the five fold ministry gifts. This book will make advancement in the Kingdom and it will bring an endless dichotomy that will bring many into kingdom alignment. As your Spiritual Mother, Son I have watched your struggle with the passion to soar and birth this book. It has come into fruition and will be a beacon of light as it inspires nations.

Dr. Polly Elliot, International Mother, Chief Apostle & a Kingdom Dominion Governors of Key 2 the Kingdom International Covenant Communion Inc. Kinston, NC

Behold the Hand of God, The Right Hand of Fellowship In A Left Handed World is a must read for those who hunger for finding their place in the body of Christ. The hand of the ready writer, Archbishop Kenneth D. Grimble has provided the body of Christ a Manuel for Kingdom Alignment & Kingdom Authority.

Lee Arthur L. Crawford, Senior Pastor of Cathedral of Praise Christian Center Springfield, IL

Many great organizations were built on the word of God, and Christian values. With a thorough background check, you will discover they have left the foundation their founders had in mind and have gone along that of humanism and even the occult. Some of our major universities and even denominations have slid so far from the foundation they were built on the founders wouldn't recognize it. We have many Christian based organizations that have literally disguised their name by abdicating from the faith to be politically correct instead of standing up for whom they believe in. Archbishop K. Dewayne Grimble, as a spiritual Doctor has discovered that the Church can and should be preserved by returning to the word of God and of course to God himself before it is too late. I am sure you will as I did find this book entitled," Behold the Hand of God, the Right Hand of Fellowship In A Left Handed World," informative, decisive and motivational.

Archbishop Willie Bolden
Chief Apostle of Rehoboth Faith Cathedral, Inc

Behold the Hand of God, The Right Hand of Fellowship In A Left Handed World is a book of great perceptions regarding Kingdom positioning that will lead you into Kingdom Dimension. This book is a distinctive resource for your personal and ministry library.

Prophet Ricky R. Smith Sr.,
Worship Deliverance Praise Tabernacle, Inc
Springfield, IL

DEDICATION

I want to dedicate this book to first and foremost to my wife and partner in faith Lady Diane Grimble. She believed in me and stuck by my side when I know that she should have taken the first flight out. My wife has been a source of strength that propelled me to push when everything in me said to give up and quit.

Lady Diane Grimble, I not only dedicate this book to you but also I also dedicate my life to you.......you are a wonderful friend, drill instructor, lover, inspirer, motivator, wife and leader in the Kingdom of our Lord God.

I also dedicate this book to my mother, the late Bessie N. Grimble who was a pillar of strength, wisdom, knowledge and kindness in all the days of her life.

I dedicate this book to my father, Herb, brother, Kelvin, brother, Anthony, aunt, Jennie, my mother-in-law, Juanita (Momma Moore).

I dedicate this book to my daughter Amber, two sons Antawn & Marvel.

I dedicate this book to my cousins Ricky, Harold, Lamont, Jeff, Felicia, Keisha...(too many to list).

I dedicate this book to my spiritual sons and daughters.

I dedicate this book to my spiritual father Archbishop Willie Bolden.

I dedicate this book to my spiritual mother, Apostle Dr. Polly Elliot

I dedicate this book to my friends, associates and my enemies.

I dedicate this book to all my professors, instructors, leaders, teachers, mentors and spiritual advisors.

I dedicate this book to those in my inner circle (too many to list but this is for you).

I dedicate this book to each member of my family because you have played a role in my development as a Man of God.

I dedicate this book to all five fold leaders and episcopates.

I dedicate this book to my very first spiritual parents in Pastor Jerry D. Doss & Mother Curtistine Doss.

I dedicate this book to all those who desire to write but are afraid to allow the ready pen writer to come forth.

I also want to say to my Grandchildren, Ashton and Addison, you are a source of Joy and delight to me, Granddaddy Loves you dearly.

CONTENTS

PREFACE

Systematically speaking, we have realized that something is not right or currently there is something quite wrong with the status of the Church. It is so clear that there is so much more that God has in store for the body of Christ If we would just step into Kingdom Alignment. As we gaze through the portals of time, the Church continues to flourish its sacred mandate fueled by efforts of religious rhetoric. The preponderance of this religious rhetoric is best illustrated in Acts 19, when the sons of Sceva tried to imitate the vagabond Jews. During an attempt to call a demon out, the demon stated, "Jesus I know and Paul I know but who are you?" This is a classic example of current Church posture and a reality in this hour. There is a tendency to pretend or imitate what we see practiced within the Church rather than really being connected to the source, who is God. For example, we casually call the physical building where believers congregate "the Church" without any reverence for the God of the Church.

We continue to invite the presence of God into the building, yet he refuses to commune with "the Church" when "the Church" has not separated from the love of the flesh. Consider the time and season, it is imperative for Church members to individually align and "the Church" itself must corporately align with the Father's will. To gain access to the next dimension of the Father, we must become the living word in the atmosphere.

A new day of illumination has dawned on the Church, the advent of a fresh move of God to usher into a Kingdom mentality. The previous move of God was directly focused on a Church mentality, and the fresh move culminated with every seasonal stanza the Church has gone through, will focus on Kingdom Mentality. Out with the old ideologies and in with the new wine of revelation, and answers to the mysteries that shall be bestowed unto the body of Christ enabling operation in a new plateau. As the door way of the next dimension becomes increasingly decreased in breadth we must apprehend the breakers anointing(Mark 16:15-18) to breach the frozen ice of religion and religious mindset. A pseudo expression of religion has arisen, it looks like the real thing, which is relationship with God, but in essence it is an imitation without any power. Within the new dimension, religion will not be allowed to gain access. While there will be futile attempts to gain entrance, the access code for religion has been denied.

INTRODUCTION

Our society is so sin conscious that the Holy Spirit is overlooked and Overridden, which allows sin to dominate. Opposing the Holy Spirit is perpetuated by humanistic endeavor to prevent people of God from receiving their worthy portion of righteousness. In fact, many do not realize the abundance of wealth attainable of righteousness. But, a Church in direct alignment with the Word of God is likened to a key that perfectly fits a lock designed to allow entrance to vault of wealth that will release a plethora of provision for those who walk righteously before God. James 1:27 indicates, "Pure religion and undefiled before God and the Father is this: To visit the fatherless and widow in their affliction and keep himself unspotted from the world. The Church portrays the notion that all the answers are known by "the Church". But, it is clear the cylinders are not clicking because if they were the power of God would be unleashed and there would be a greater amount of miracles manifested as evidenced of the Church lining up with Kingdom Authority.

This book could be one of the missing pieces to the puzzle that will cause the Church to truly plug into the unadulterated power of God. This book discusses current and previous Church structural issues established by man without recognition that it is the Word of God that gives the body of Christ a clear concise blue print of how God's Church is supposed to be structured. This book will give you a glimpse into divine dimension of the mind of God and allow you to reflect on the present depictions of what mankind has tried to illustrate through their own understanding of God's Word. If read carefully and often this book will prove to be a useful tool that will enlighten you as you become acquainted with, "Behold the hand of God: The Right hand of fellowship in a left handed world."

Chapter 1:
The Details Do Make a Difference

How "the Church" is viewed by members and leaders makes a difference in whether the Church can be in alignment with the will of God. The details that outline Church philosophy include: religion, the physical building, the presence of God in the Church, Church leaders, leadership responsibilities, and Church members response to leadership. It is plausible to state, knowing the initial intent of God for the Church that through the eyes of the Lord God Almighty and sustainer of our soul, the view of the Kingdom of God and the Church of God is disillusioned and truly distorted providing a skewed impression of the original design. This view is far from the intent of the true and living designer who spoke his

1

word into existence. If the truth be told about the present condition of "the Church", Jesus Christ would walk by the majority of edifices and say, "I am not welcomed in the Church which I created." Our society would better characterize the present representation of "the Church" as an organism where the creator is removed from his own body. How do we summarize that the creator of the Church is not welcomed in the Church? Simply, that the spirit of error brings about an unrealistic façade of religious acts that persuade some nonbelievers and believers toward an unprecedented notion that they have access to heavenly provisions. Mainline Church spectators feel access is granted to the body of Christ just because access is granted to the physical building in which the Church roster bears their signature.

Many present day Church attendees feel they are connected to the Church because they make efforts to attend a physical building every Sunday. This notion is precipitated by such theological doctrines as Hyper-Calvinism, Polytheism, Monotheism and a host of other false doctrines. Moreover, "the Church" has been hood-winked with a diabolical plot to bring humanistic endeavors into the spiritual arena to pawn them off as new revelation. 2Timothy 3:5 indicates "Having the form of godliness, but denying the power thereof: From such turn away." The sincere evidence of this scripture indicates people in the world must embrace Jesus Christ through a divine relationship. Lip service is insufficient as it will only serve as a religious shell, liken to speaking the word of God without allowing the power of God to flow through like an electrical cord plugged into an outlet. In other words, professing righteousness through a connection with the Church building yet functioning with no power or authority.

The present day perception of the Church building has hindered many from understanding the difference between relationship and religion. The mere gesture of equating religion to righteousness is a strong indicator that society and the devil are intertwined and inseparable without desire to be severed. This façade has gone on long enough and has crept into the Church deeply infecting the plans for the kingdom of God. Needless to say, the Church has abdicated further from the tenets of truth. The enemy has strategically prepared a new breed of diabolical leaders who have been trained and schooled in theology from some of the most prestigious seminaries and biblical colleges across the country. There is a false presumption that a well prepared seminary graduate is a far better candidate to lead the flock of God than a candidate that has labored in the word and presence of God. It is evident that some attend seminaries and bible colleges only to further a satanic agenda to deter people away from the plan and will of God. Although education is good, it will never take the presence of the best teacher, the Holy Spirit. Likewise, it grieves the Holy Spirit to allow the flesh to be appeased by those exhibiting religious precedence rather than by those who have been prepared through intense training while maintaining an intimate relationship with God during the process.

While it is true that our society frowns against preachers that have not been trained theologically, it is also true and an indictment against God to presume that every seminary or bible college graduate has a relationship with God. In our current demise of Church polity, some Churches rather recruit from seminaries rather than look from within a pool of qualified candidates from highly recommended referral networks to lead the Church. Societal peer pressure propels believers into embracing a notion that preachers must be trained theologically in order to be effective leaders. Everyone needs to be trained for their profession of choice. However, the training regiment should be developed by the leaders who are providing oversight. College may not be an alternative for every preacher. It should be noted that some may need some an intense level of training with particular emphasis on reading and speaking the word of God. Furthermore, it is important that each candidate for leadership have a prayer life and strong study habits to have a balanced perspective. Recently, on a news cast dealing with religious immorality, a pastor who had been theologically trained was interviewed by at Television Program. During the interview the interviewee stated he not only served as a pastor but did not believe in the God that he preached about. Due to a lack of discernment, the members of this local Church did not have a clue their leader held no belief in God. Consequently, studies reveal many others have misrepresented themselves as Church leaders but deny belief in the God. Societal peer pressure has also resulted in placing men and women unqualified spiritually as members of Church decision making boards in desperation to feel the a void in leadership. Consequently, the rush to get someone with business acumen has put the wrong people in positions of authority. This is a classical model of a wolf in sheep's clothing misleading the flock of God to further his demonic agenda, and the blind leading the blind into the fiery flames of hell. We must understand concisely that the Church has embraced a deformed posture through entertaining a spirit of deception.

The spirit of deception continues to coexists and linger in the Church but no one has been able to discern it is a demonic spirit. In fact, there are Church members who do not believe in the existence of demonic spirits. But, we are living in a time where everyone needs a dose of truth. We need to understand that spiritual warfare exists and the devil is real. It is also a necessity to understand the nature of delegated authority. Almighty God gave the devil delegated authority. And, the process by which we empower the devil is having doubt in the infallible word of God. Also, disobedience is another critical element which contributes further to the demise of the Church. While thriving to coexist with a deformed posture the Church attempts to imitate the true body of Christ.

Since the world embraces this counterfeit version of the true living Church, a unrighteous seed deposited cannot reproduce a seed for righteousness. The problem with Church formation is leaders continue to desire the benefits of righteousness while living according to the tenets of the world, and teaching Church members to do the same. Given the prevalent Church polity and familiarity, the Church is operating on a religious basis rather than in a righteous manner, which is rebellion. I Samuel 15:23 states: For rebellion is as the sin of witchcraft, and stubbornness is as iniquity and idolatry. Because thou hast rejected the word of the LORD, he hath also rejected thee from being king. This New Age world and the scientific characteristics that it lives by fails to honor or accept the precepts that Christ left for his Church. Instead of walking and embracing the victory Christ left the Church, the present the image of the Church looks like a victim. This image of the Church has expanded primarily by the iconic figures of celebrities who dampen the true nature of Christ and weaken holiness with a watered down version of Christianity.

Christianity has taken the back seat in the mindset of the people. In other words, it is a mere attempt of the humanistic mind to be influenced by those who possess wealth which is utilized to subvert others to adopt a new age concept of success which is indicative of a faulty spiritual prowess. This attempt is part of the demonic agenda to establish a new ideology of Christianity without any form of righteousness and to catapult the agenda to those who desire to have the same success with a new age God. It is easy to follow someone who has success by the world standards because the world views success without God. This new age perspective reverts us back to the days of old when Nimrod felt he could be a better God than our original true and living self-eternal and self-existing God.

Throughout the discourse of history, we have seen created beings such as Lucifer, Adam, and Nimrod each having a desire to be like God or to replace God. This visual preview of the creature trying to take the place of the creator is nothing new. The famed movie Frankenstein portrayed a mad scientist who created a freak of nature through the exploits of scientific research and the pursuit of becoming the creature's creator. This new age perspective is stemmed from the days of Lucifer trying to take the creative virtue from the Lord, as the mad scientist did with Frankenstein. A current realistic example is the new scientific ideology involving the process of human and animal cloning. The scientific creativity potential has permeated the hearts and minds of our modern day scientists who have the desire to become well-known in the academic arena. However, the desire for fame has become a quest to be like God. The mere comparison is just a query of ludicrous attempts of a finite mind trying to be equal to the infinite mind of God.

Instead of trying to be like God, it would be much more of a progressive endeavor if the believers would plug into God to embrace the greatest of source of power that exist in the world. If these men would look at God in the same likeness of an electrical cord being plugged into a socket, there would be such a joy in being connected and converted from a deceptive source that carries no power whatsoever. The reflection is very similar to the present Church and the body of Christ. Although the two have similar facets, they are extremely different in the true source of power often likened to two negative plugs being hooked to one another. In this context, we know that the two negative shall not be connected. As evidence, the religious Church and the body of Christ shall not be connected.

Chapter 2:
The Divine Formation

The body of Christ is the manifestation of individual parts coming together aligned for sole the purpose of allowing the power of god to flow through and eradicate sin. James 5:20 states "Let him know that he which converted the sinner from the error of his way, shall save a soul from death, and shall hide a multitude of sins. This is ultimately the primary purpose of the Church and we have failed so miserably.   To accomplish the purpose outreach or evangelism is required. However, the Church does not understand the importance for outreach or evangelism. In fact, many do not understand there is a difference between the two. Outreach exist as a platform to reach out to the masses of people who have needs that must be met through such venues as community centers, or urban development corporations. These venues provide services and products through individual donations, corporate donations, corporate sponsorships or grants to help those in need. Evangelism, on the other hand, is the stirring up of the word of God into the lives of the people to draw them into the Kingdom of God through a divine relationship with God. In a concerted effort, the indelible details of corporate evangelism have become a lost art in the Church because of fear perpetuated by gangs, and other elements of criminal nature. The Church is commonly associated with both outreach and evangelism, but given the substructure of the Church when compared to the Leaning Tower of Pisa one must wonder, tilted so much to the right when will it literally fall. Nevertheless, the word "Church" has been so overused without clear understanding. The Greek word for Church is "ecclesia", which means to be called out of darkness into the marvelous light. Those called out seems to be missing in action because many view the Church as a literal joke. The response to this query is primarily due to a close examination of Church in the same light as the wheat and tare. Because there is a problem in identifying the difference between wheat and tare, the world can no longer tell the difference between those in the Church and

12

those in the world. The disparity in examining members of the Church and those visiting for the initial time is just amazing. A familiar spirit that invades the Church service and tries to mimic everything that is being done will need to be exposed and eradicated.

Even though the counterfeit spirit tries to raise its head up every now and then, it must be sought out and destroyed. Contrary to popular belief, the fleshy shell that many identify as the Church is just a false replica of the true image that God expressed in His word. We must be able to present ourselves as a living sacrifice, holy and acceptable to the Lord. The body of Christ was unequivocally designed to stand tall, and walk in divine authority, to be a body of believers identified as those called out of darkness into the marvelous light. Exodus 14:13 states," And Moses said unto the people, Fear ye not, stand still and see the salvation of the Lord, which he will show you to-day: for the Egyptians whom ye have seen to-day, you shall see them again no more for-ever. The mentality of some Christian leaders is the kingdom represents a byproduct of the Church as oppose to the correct view that Church is a product of the kingdom.

In order to effectively adapt as a bondservant, the Church must embrace a kingdom mindset, a kingdom connection, and kingdom authority. The spirit of error is a cousin to the spirit of truth in that even the devil uses it to gain membership in his kingdom. The spirit of error has also tried to enter into the apostolic dimension illegally without much success. Although the enemy has used a counterfeit endorsement to appear authentic, it failed to a make an effective mark. We must admonish this notion that natural realm does not have intercourse with the spiritual realm. Whenever there is a violation of the spiritual principle, the problem can become monumental in size. According to 2 Samuel 21:16," And Ishbibenob, which was of the sons of giants, the weight of whose spear weighed three hundred shekels of brass in weight, he being girded with a new sword thought to have slain David."

While some have tried to nullify the existence of giants, there is living proof of a nation of giants as a result of the union of giants and humans. Before the angels could engage in the act of intercourse, the giants had to ask permission. This is an invasion of the principle of the natural and spiritual realm intermingling. Within every born again believer, there is an intermingling of the Holy Spirit and humanity. This has been defined by theologians as a homeostatic union. This would not be a violation

14

with God because He is the creator and his plan takes precedence over natural laws. In other words, the devil tries to gain access into the arena where he has no access. It is like a key and a lock model, every key does not fit. Every now and then, the key may fit but it may not turn the cylinders.

The devil violated heavenly principles and he was evicted out of perfection to become the king of darkness and prince of the air. Because of the fall of Adam in the Garden of Eden, this endeavor opened a portal for the devil to gain access to world which is in a fallen state. Let us examine Chapter 3 verse 1 of the Book of Genesis where man initially fell: Now the serpent was more subtle than any beast of the field which the Lord God had made. And he said unto the woman yea, hath God said, ye shall not eat of every tree of the garden? The trickery of the enemy admonishes us to see how the devil used the serpent to beguile eve to eat of the tree of life of the Garden of Eden. The fact that the enemy had access indicates that he was granted delegated authority. The serpent deceptively implied that God did not want her to eat so that she could not benefit from being as a God if she would eat of the fruit. The rebellious act was not concluded until Eve gave the fruit to Adam and partook of the fruit.

Adam tried to reason fruitlessly with God because Adam did not see anything happen to Eve once she partook of the fruit. Because of this reasoning, Adam decided to go against the holy orders that were given to him by God. Genesis 3:1-7, the fall of mankind took place and caused a wedge to take place between creator and creation. Each one who participated in this fall, God punished them accordingly. Man was punished to work by the sweat of his brow. Woman was given the curse of bringing life into this world. The serpent was given punishment to be on its belly. The fall of mankind had spiraling effect on the plan and will of the creator. As the creator, He foreknew that this act of disobedience would take place. He had an ace in the hole that he pulled out of the eons of time. This counteraction would allow mankind to be restored through a regenerative process called the plan salvation. In the plan of Salvation, God purposed to send a portion of Himself in the Word of God, wrapped himself in humanity and come in the world through a sent woman of God by the name of Mary. Mary, a virgin woman full of the Holy Spirit was sent with this assignment to be used for a miraculous birth called the Immaculate Conception. In other words, God would supernaturally through His omnipotence come into a woman's womb and impregnate her without having intercourse and allow a child to born to a chosen woman that was espoused to a man who had not consummated their relationship.

This created a major problem for Joseph and the people in their surrounding area to find his wife pregnant in which he had not been intimate with her. Joseph had the right to have Mary stoned to death. However, Joseph had a visitation by an angel sent with a message from God. He was clearly blown away that his espoused wife was chosen to carry the seed of God to be a savior to the world. Joseph was designated the first step father to the only begotten son of God. It is clear that the Church needs to abandon the mentality that it is ok to sin and to practice it. However, there are key figures in the Church who have adopted questionable practices and principles that were in the old testament to justify their actions. One of those questionable principles is called the Kingdom Now principle where married men or women of God may have the propensity to have casual sex with multiple counterparts to satisfy their sexual needs. The premise in this example is that a husband or wife needs more than one partner to satisfy all of their sexual needs. In concert, the concept precipitates that husband or wife can act on their desires and feed the need. The spirit of lust has been around the Church since the goddess of fertility was presented. Nimrod, the grandson of Shem, was noted strongly because he slept with his mother in law and the lust demon was released in the atmosphere. Furthermore, the spirit of sexual deviations was spewed out into the atmosphere and the foundation of Christ had been overlooked. Because of this tainted pattern of activity, the Church has been hindered in their efforts to move into a new dimension.

Nimrod was a copy cat artist who wanted to be a God. Although it was an impossible task, Nimrod felt a need to build the Tower of Babel to be close to God. However, nimrod refused to live the lifestyle that would further his efforts into righteousness. Needless to say, nimrod desired that righteous would be directed towards him instead of directing the quest to our heavenly father who most assuredly deserves the reverence. Nimrod's quest to receive the reverence was promulgated by his desire to be God. How foolish could he have been to think he could take the place of the risen savior or the almighty God? Men like nimrod and Lucifer seek to be

God without possessing the correct nature to accomplish this endeavor. Both men have different characteristics that would not allow the spiritual nature of omnipotence or omnipresence to coexist in the flesh. This is a serious complex of sin that aides unbelievers to develop a quest for self preservation instead of a God preservation. In order to line up with God who created everything for his benefit, we must eradicate sin and understand our purpose.

The bible says in Ephesians 4:16,"From whom the whole body fitly joined together and compacted by that which every joint supplieth, according to the effectual working in the measure of every part, maketh increase of the body unto the edifying of itself in love. From the cosmic standpoint, this is a command for the body of Christ to come together for the perfecting of the body of Christ. Individual parts cannot nor will not give the creator glory in its endeavor to do his will without connecting with others in the body of Christ. The bible also indicates no man or no one is an island. This pattern precipitates a cultic behavior which does not glorify the plan and will of God. In this hour, we have for a task at hand to break all denominational vices to cause the body to draw together so we can draw nigh to the father. Our minds have prompted us through fleshly vices to keep the Church separated. In other words, the devil has slipped through the cracks and widened it for other demonic overtures to have access. We must learn to close all portals so that the enemy does not gain access. To do so, the Church must focus on teaching deliverance and spiritual warfare.

Chapter 3:

The Missing Pieces to the Puzzle

We live in a throw away type society which is fueled by a mindset of divide and conquer. In addition, our society is one premised to operating strictly on humanistic endeavor. According to St James 1:8," a double minded man is unstable in all his ways." We must be careful for those who have a double mindset when it comes to the things of God. Romans 8:7 states, "Because the carnal mind is enmity against God: for it is not subject to the law of God, neither indeed can be." The creature has made futile attempt that the creature has made futile attempts to realign with the creator but these attempts have been unsuccessful. Just as keys are designed to open a lock, mankind has failed in its humanistic efforts to gain access to heaven.

The eyes of the learned must become acclimated to the eyes of the Lord. In order for the Church to reconnect with the resurrected power, there must be a falling away from religion. Religion cripples believer's or at least stagnates them from real pursuit of an unadulterated relationship with Jesus Christ. Many new age Churches have adopted concepts of having a relationship with God the creator but no belief in Jesus Christ as the Son of God. Religion is a vague expression of a Christian impression that implies that a new believer has been granted eternal life without connecting with Jesus Christ.

There are some doctrines such as Hyper-Calvinism (more commonly referred to as eternal security) that emphasize that each believer can still commit sin and maintain an authentic relationship with Jesus Christ. Needless to say, this doctrine or dogma has spurned many debates and arguments which further separate the cosmic body of believers from uniting for the purpose of building the Kingdom of Heaven. There are doctrines of devils that have invaded the Church and propelling them to jump in bed with the enemy. Our society tends to embrace some efforts of the enemy out of need to be connected to faulty beliefs without understanding the plight of spiritual warfare that has been released. The nature of sin continues to rise in our nation to the point that our nation has fallen short of Gods Standards. The Church is altruistically allowing the spirit of truth to be compromised with the spirit of error. Although both have existed through the eons of time, the Word of God has always prevailed. The New Age campaigners facilitate strong efforts to create awareness of new religious movements. The stagnant Church must reflect on the previous patterns of righteousness presented as evidence of the Churches posture as being marginal through sin.

Because humanistic endeavors have invaded the Church in such a monumental way, the average Church attendee would not be able to decipher the differences of a Church sanctioned by man from a Church sanctioned by the Holy Spirit. If we gather a closer look at the presentation of the Church, we shall find a flawed perspective of the Church and Church discourse for which it has taken. Because the Church has chosen to abort the original blue print, the end result is a reproach against the Church's identity. In other words, God established His blue print and we have the audacity to alter His plan because we don't understand. Proverbs 3:5 states, "Trust in the lord with all thy heart; and lean not unto your own understanding." The scripture implies that no matter how smart we become; but, we are also relegated to know that it is impossible to be smarter than our creator. We must understand that our creators mind operates limitlessly in a sphere unprecedented by the human mind. The human side has limitations that relegate us on a level that cannot compete or comprehend the magnitude of the unparalleled mindset of our heavenly fathers. The nature of sin conditions an individual into thinking they can hang around the word by attending Church, but not allow the Church to dwell on the inside of them.

2 Chronicles 7:14 states, "If my people, which are called by my name, shall humble themselves, and pray, and seek my face, and turn from their wicked ways; then will I hear from heaven, and will forgive their sins, and will hear their land." This scripture gives directions to sinners and believers, but the problem most believers have a loss of direction. Too many Christians get caught in the emotions of music, and singing songs hoping that God will turn their situation around. It is purely amazing that a vocalist can use a song that may sound good, but the pattern of the song is written with the wrong principle. We must be mindful that while the lyrics may

sound good, the lyrics may have a humanistic application instead of one spiritually compliant as a solution. In one stanza, the songwriter is obligated to apply the word of God in his writings. In one song it implies that God will turn your situation around and the musician tell those in the audience to turn around in a 360 degree turn. The problem is the instructions in that Song place the hearer in the same position you began.

Although this is a sincere song, its application gives improper instructions. Instead the song writer should have said that God wants you to go the opposite direction in which they had been directed. However, if we look at the scripture in 2 Chronicles 7:14, which says.......... turn from their wicked ways....." does not mean that you start on one position and end in the same position. On the contrary, the Bible depicts that we must turn away from the sin of wickedness and move toward the opposite direction towards righteousness. But, many will stay in sin or straddle the fence. The abdication from righteousness has presented the present Church as lukewarm because the world now views the Church as an entertainment venue. Many believers desire to only attend a Church that is driven by music or that has a celebrity as the visionary. While music is a great tool to draw people into the Church and it plays a great role in Worship and Praise, we must be mindful that the Holy Spirit is an enabler to the process of creating the atmosphere where miracles can take place. Similarly, the Church has become a major business that is permeated by the personality of the visionary. In other words, the people will only attend if the visionary is present. Even though the visionary is a vital part of the Church, the progression of this Church should not be hindered because the visionary could be on another assignment.

The bible speaks of a leader who leaves the 99 to go pursue after the 1. It would be preposterous for anyone to think that this leader in Matthew 18:12 would leave the other sheep (99) in the hands of an under-shepherd (lead elder with his vision) while he go pursue after the one that has left. A typical Church is hindered with this erroneous one man system that the doors are shut if the leader is not available. Although this man or woman may be the visionary, this ministry does not belong to them. It is essential that Churches train up and use the elders to assist while the visionary is on another assignment. No man is an island and we must have an understanding of the intent of his plan. It is all too often that man carries the vision but, he or she is under delegated authority of

God. We need to understand that accountability is essential and Biblical when God gives a vision to his chosen candidate. While accountability is the missing ingredient in Churches today, there are so many leaders abdicating to standing alone in this hour. While clergymen make it hard for true spiritual parents who are walking in spiritual enlightenment and truth, there are also those who abandon the need for spiritual accountability.

Although many Clergy come from different theological perspectives and are committed to their school of thought, it is a necessity that these men of God become more connected to the almighty creator than to the information in which the school of theology purports. It is apparent that the body of Christ has been burned tremendously with the veracity of theological assertions. In fact, these assertions have promulgated a wider gap resulting in a tremendous need for the walls of separation to come down. Further evidence related to the lack of accountability is that a new school of thought propels leaders to abandon the need for spiritual parents. However, there are many leaders that have been abused by those parents who were unlearned or who were extremely abusive in the legalistic approach to parenting.

27

In addition to poor parenting, there is a tremendous need for spiritual mentors in this hour. Although we must understand that there is a difference, a mentor is not the same as a spiritual parent. A mentor is one who imparts knowledge into the protégés life. One the other hand, the spiritual parent illumination comes from a term described as the Malachi Mandate that is extracted from the last verse of the Old Testament.

The Bible says in Malachi 4:6, "And he (God) shall turn the heart of the father to the children, and the heart of the children to their fathers, lest I come and smite the earth with a curse. While many people establish membership in the local assembly, they fail to realize in so doing they become spiritual children to their senior leaders who are set over as caretakers of the flock. This does not endorse the current posture of two headed freak or monster that is employed in the concept of pastor and co-pastor. The bible speaks about fatherhood in I Corinthians 4:15, "For though ye have ten thousand instructors in Christ, yet have ye not many fathers: for in Christ Jesus I have begotten you through the gospel." While looking at scripture in Old Testament and New Testament, we are succinctly clear that God made some leaders spiritual parents over his spiritual children. The problem increasingly expands to extreme levels as the local level spiritual parents try to take the glory from God who is the ultimate father of all. Spiritual Parents are essential for a balanced perspective in leading a flock. While the Church has been established to view the set visionary as the spiritual father, there is a new radical move that refutes the need for spiritual parents. The indelibly notion is that they are connected to God and don't need a human to cover them. This posture refutes the Malachi mandate and furthermore places the Church in a bastardized mentality. Fear and abuse have purported this pattern because of the abusive leadership styles of former leadership. In other words, God has established true leaders to be examples to their spiritual children and not to have a heavy handed approach as one standing on their necks to control them.

Likewise, God wants us to live such a progressive lifestyle that they will heed to embrace the sincere Word of God. Abuse and control has filtered through some portals of ministries, networks or fellowship that were prompted by eager new organizations as a recruitment endeavor. This type of negative pattern gives some leaders a sense of gratification to be out in the forefront. The brevity of these newly established organizations is centered around recruitment strategies for these new organizations. They sell the positions of episcopacy as an effort to increase the size of their organization. Validation of their organization is predicated on the number of episcopates and the number Churches to bring into their organization. Often times, these men or women get very little or no training to fulfill this position of oversight. Without reverence for this sacred office of the Bishop, these people will look like they really have the training needed to fulfill this position but in essence they have no idea of the merits of this office. Furthermore, the term episcopacy is defined as an organization managed or run by episcopates. In other words, they want to become administrators without any knowledge of how to administrate. Now we can see how the Church has been hindered by placing people in positions that have not been properly prepared or that left their previous organization in the wrong spirit.

The office of the Bishop is not a calling as noted in the five functions listed in Ephesians 4th chapter. However, some try to use the connotation of this administrative office as that of an elder or pastor. Bishops are administratively appointed and their assignment is not directly linked to any other function. Many try to embrace it primarily because it is a desired office. In everything that God created, he presented protocol based on Genesis 1:11 and 12. Needless to say, it falls into a category where a person's responsibilities expands beyond the scope of a singular Church. In other words, he or she must be able to administrate effectively an individual Church before one can expand to a wider spectrum of Churches. The fact that Paul did not include women in this capacity because the signs of the time indicated women were treated unfairly in their particular cultural. Women were considered indentured slaves in some different cultures.

Chapter 4:

The Gears of Religion Are Not Working

The present posture of the Church is currently deformed. As a result, the deformation process continues to abdicate further from the original plan of God. The current demise of the Church has been contingent on the notion that many people attend a Church building but, does not indicate that a Church attendee is a born again believer. This mindset continues to grow at an alarming rate and it is a direct detriment to the plan and will of God. Our heavenly father gave the true Church a plan of action that would restore the fallen nature back to right standing and right alignment. In other words, the enemy had been given access because of the fall of Adam.

This pattern of thinking would construe that the Adamic nature was the falling nature where mankind could identify that sin existed and was the main cause for the hindrance in God having a relationship with his creation. Because of the continued deviation from the plan of God, there appears to be no valid stance for inhabitants of earth to read or write about anything during the 400 years of silence rendered between the last book of the Old Testament (Malachi) and the first book of the New Testament (Matthew).

Even though this period was construed to be a time that God indicated he would be silent, mankind decided to write material and say that it came from God. The fact men wrote the Apocrypha during this period of silence furthering the speculation that man has attempted to pawn information without the authorization of God. Man has taken the approach that God has done it already and there is no need to do anything else. The doctrine of Hyper-Calvinism purports that man can continually sin and the sins are forgiven by the Jesus Christ's death, burial and resurrection. This particular religious hypothesis has been deemed eternal security. This popular approach to reasoning from an intellectual standpoint has been referred to in the scholastic circles as Hyper-Calvinism. It is purported under their teachings is that you cannot loose your salvation regardless of sin, and the effects of sin. 2 Thessalonians 3:6 states, "Now we command you, brethren, in the name of our Lord Jesus Christ, that ye withdraw yourselves from every brother that walketh disorderly, and not after the traditions which he received of us."

For instance, the word "disorderly" means out of order; not at one's post of duty; undisciplined; irregular; lawless and disorderly. They act accordingly to their own will, intellect, ideology or mindset, or thinking pattern. Paul says that he did not go out of his rank or post of duty, but kept his places as a true and tried soldier of Jesus Christ. We must understand that many have bought into this Calvinist message because their philosophy allows you to think that they have benefits from salvation in spite of being under the Adamic nature. The mindset comprised here would allude to the notion that a spirit of delusion had seeped into the mainstream of the Christian arena. The bible says in Isaiah 66:4, "I also will choose their delusions, and will bring their fears upon them; because when I called, none did answer; when I spake, they did not hear: but they did evil before mine eyes, and chose that in which I delighted not. In 2 Thessalonians

2:11 & 12, "And for this cause God shall send them strong delusion, that they should believe a lie:' Because mankind has continued to refuse to hear and fear God, they have clearly chosen not to get a clear understanding of the heartbeat of God. They have chosen their own delusion's which is to embrace a lie or opinion that is the opposite of the word of God.

In addition to the delusions, God would also bring fears upon them. God has been talking to both his real members and the unsaved, but those of the religious Church do not answer and continue doing evil before his eyes do what he disdains. This is the pattern of the false Church to appear to follow the ideology of his word but cannot embrace his spirit because he does not dwell on the inside of them. There is always a preponderance of the creation saying that God knows there heart. The problem with the religious Church is that they cannot hear him because they can only receive what is read to them by His Word. The religious Church needs to come alive through the power of the spirit of the living God that they all might be damned who believe not the truth but have pleasure in unrighteousness. There is a true saying, "a mind is a terrible thing to waste." The natural mindset has the tendency to embrace unrighteousness to think that

36

God will be merciful in reaching out to those who practice sin. Although the sinner nature is alive and well, we must understand we can live in this life without sinning. As hard as it may be to believe, it is possible for us not to sin. However, if we do sin we have an advocate that will stand in the gap who will take our sin away. Through the process of repentance, we can receive a clean slate and no longer have to allow the nature of sin to reign. In other words, they will embrace the mindset of a sinner and say we have all sinned. Most saints will convey a message that says "I am a sinner saved by Grace".

The mission of one who has embraces salvation is to condition the heart, mind and body to be in obedience to his word. The difference in this mindset is that if or when one sin, they can repent through true repentance. In this case, the sin consciousness has been taken away because the saint dwells in Christ Jesus. Instead of thinking like a sinner, we think like a saint through the power of the holy spirit. This altered mindset gives us the assurance that God is moving by his spirit. The Bible says in Leviticus 11:44, " For I am the Lord your God: Ye shall be holy; for I am holy: neither shall ye defile yourselves with any manner of creeping thing that creepeth upon the earth."

The finite mind of mankind is an instrument for retaining information which is used and applied with principles useful for living an eventful life from a humanistic standpoint. As we delve further into the finite mindset, we ascertain that reasoning is a process where logic can take root, and decision making becomes its expression. It is a shame that there is a contradicting pattern evolving where the devil has invaded the Church through the religious preacher who has forsaken the responsibility of pursuing an intimate relationship.

Many of these leaders make efforts to gain access to Churches through diabolical efforts such attending bible colleges and/or seminaries to gain knowledge and understanding of scripture. Recently, evidence has surfaced that points a horrendous light on preachers who live loosely from the standards of righteousness. More indictments have been levied upon the Church because preachers are living religiously, pretending to be saved. Preachers are smoking and/or selling dope, and there is and there is a proclivity of leaders involved in lascivious lifestyles such as pornography, fornication, adultery, homosexuality and bestiality. The efforts of these men deceiving God's children and preying on them as a lamb sacrificed as unto a wolf, angers God tremendously to deceive his children and to prey on them as a lamb sacrificed as unto a wolf. The burden intensifies as the need for prayer is essential for the carnal Church to wake up so that they can hear from God. The carnal Church is one that cannot discern nor hear from God. The Bible says in Romans 8:7, "Because the carnal mind is enmity against God: for it is not subject to the law of God, neither indeed can be." The latter part of the above mentioned scripture indicates that a carnal mind (that is a mind that has not been connected to our creator by divine relationship) does not have the ability to commune with God. With all the foolishness that the enemy has promulgated into the body of Christ, we must be mindful of the deceptive tricks the enemy has done. Presently there are many preachers sitting in prison due to their affinity with ungodly practices.

The present stanza with the Church concerning the nature of sin has been watered down tremendously. The bible says in Proverbs 27:5 says, "open rebuke is greater than secret love." This particular act should be the last result when training and equipping leaders within the Church. Our focus should be to build people with a Kingdom message granted by the Power of God. It has come to light that many don't believe the devil is real and that wickedness prevails because of the devil's the deeds. Evil continues to exist because individuals who pretend to be believers have refused to access their spiritual powers from above or they don't have the understanding or just don't have required access code to gain entrance. Our society is so fickle because they are quick to allow media and movie industry to release witchcraft to access the masses but are oppose to promoting Jesus Christ to the masses unless something drastic has occurred.

In underestimating the effects of demonic infiltration, our society has fueled the efforts of demons without truly understanding the damage it has done to the Kingdom of God. The effects of this mindset have given us many examples of demonic forces in action. The April 20, 1999 Littleton, Colorado School Massacre and the April 16, 2007, Virginia's University massacre are just a few examples where the enemy has demonically infected the victim to perform horrendous acts of injustice. This is also a great indicator how the devil has seduced children and influenced them to do such an ungodly acts as what occurred at education establishments. The enemy has continuously gained access primarily due to a world granting the key or combination to their access points. The Bible says in Matthew 11:12 "And from the days of

John the Baptist until now the Kingdom of Heaven suffereth violence, and the violent take it by force". We have become a society focused on knowledge about God instead of developing relationship with the God of the word. The dullness of the religious Churches spiritual antenna's has allowed religious Churches to move further from God instead of drawing closer to him. Truth is now being sanctioned by various select denomination's rather than being plugged into the creator. The seriousness of this matter is far beyond opinions of mankind. The bible says in Romans 1:28, "And even they did not like to retain God in their knowledge, God gave them over to a reprobate mind to do those things which are not convenient. This is something that average believer needs to realize that God will release his wrath on those who toy with the Holy Spirit. The Bible gives us further instructions in 2 Corinthian's 5-7 "Examine yourselves, whether ye be in the faith; prove your own selves. Know ye not your own selves, how that Jesus Christ is in you, except ye be reprobate's; But I trust that ye shall know that we are not reprobates; Now I pray to God that ye do no evil, no that we should appear approved, but that ye should do that which is honest, though we be as reprobates."

The scriptures above request that each of us examine ourselves whether we be in the faith and to prove that you are lining up with the Word. Paul also s States that we should know that Jesus Christ dwells in you if you invited Him into your life unless you be a reprobate. Paul also states that we know that Jesus Christ in you if you invited Him into your life, unless you are a reprobate. Paul also informs us that we know the benefits of righteousness and the power of the Holy Spirit so we refrain from becoming a reprobate. Paul instructs us to pray to God on our behalf that we do no evil because evil would separate us from God. Though we shall be tested and proved through our faith in the word of God, we should continue to examine ourselves because of the sin nature referenced to be as reprobates.

In 2 Corinthians 12:4, the bible says, "For though he was crucified through weakness, yet he liveth by the power of God. For we also are weak in him, but we shall live with him by the power of God toward you." This scripture indicates we are not to operate in our own strength, but should welcome the power of God to flow through us. We should embrace the word of God accented by the power of the Holy Ghost activated by faith from the believer. Our faith in God grants us the privilege to have access to Him before he does anything. So many believers have allowed their faith to dissipate because they want things from God, rather than pursuing a relationship with him.

Chapter 5:

My Grace is Sufficient

Do we still believe sin is a deterrent to the Church? What are the consequences of disobedience? The premise of this Book entitled, "Behold the Hand of God: The Right Hand of Fellowship in a Left Handed World" was inspired by God, because the Church is indelibly out of alignment. The scripture has several translations for the word "right" and the usage of the term "right hand" ranges from a direction to the opposite of wrong, what is just or what conforms to an established standard, and to a place of honor or authority. There must be a press toward living holy, which applies to disobedient leaders and laypeople some people will continue to be disobedient rather than embrace Gods remedy to attain righteousness. Grace has been defined as unmerited Favor by God. Because of his grace, we have a choice to plug into him.

Although God has been gracious in his redemption endeavor many people will not embrace his kind gesture of love. This paradigm denotes that the Church is presently operating far from the creator's intended plan. The predicament results in a false perception that leaders are totally responsible for the sheep learning to hear from God for themselves. But, the flock of God is also bears responsibility in learning to hear God and to know God in an intimate manner as well.

The bible says in John 10:27, "My sheep hears my voice, I know them and they follow me." It is fully clear that the religious Church does not hear from God nor has the ability to discern the heart of their leader. Whether a disobedient leader or a lay person living beneath the provision of God, the bible indicates God has better provisions for believers. The Bible says in 1 Peter 1:16, "Be ye holy because I am holy." The standard of righteousness must be adhered to in order to meet the progressiveness of the plan and will of God. In spite of this, some people will continue to be disobedient but, there is a remedy to attain righteousness. Previous generation had a stiff necked approach to their disposition and beliefs. The Church has come to a crossroads: Getting back to basics or move forward into a progressive dimension of God. It is so obvious that the Church must be reformed. As an outsider looking in through eyes of a mere man, the average religious believer would think that nothing is wrong. This reflection permeates the need for abatement from the carnal realm and move toward an abyss of the spiritual dimension.

A reformation of the Church is most vital and extremely important towards advancement of the cosmic Church. A reform shall not take place until a victory over the flesh and the spirit of mankind. The root meaning "Re-Form, can be understood as the improvement improving by alteration, correction of error, or removal of defects and faults" It means to reprove in conduct and character to "abolish or malpractice in causing a person to abandon irresponsible and immoral practices and change for the better. As we examine the Church's discourse, the membership of the Church has fought change tremendously by the ones who say they want change. It appears that most are fascinated with the idea for change but in reality they never move beyond the idea. The focus here has been merely looking at disobedience and the effect it is has on the Church. The bible profoundly speaks about the right hand of God so much more than it speaks about the left hand. This in no manner depict God as a one handed bandit. Contrary to popular belief, the hand of God is grace personified for the Church. It is epitomized by the very hand of God. The fact that we are made in His image gives us the notion of the number of five as a numerical symbol for grace.

As we look at the functions noted in Ephesians the fourth chapter, we clearly can ascertain that those functions were a distinction of a particular function rather than a mere gesture of an anointing. While there is an erroneous teaching concept of an apostle, this false teaching expresses that this one function has the other four embodied within the call. This ideology has done two dastard thing. The first is to make the call of an apostle something the violates scripture and the other is to make our God to appear schizophrenic. The calling of God was a specific mandate to epitomize his presence within the local Church. However, men and women, trying to embody all five functions into one individual. Each function is tailor made by God for an individual. Embracing truth and understanding of the operation of the function's or anointing has widened the gap of disparity. We believe that each function brings a needed value and that value keeps us in line with scripture. 1 Corinthian 7:20 says, " Let every man abide in the same calling wherein he was called. This also coincides with Genesis 1:12," And the earth brought forth grass, and herb yielding seed after his kind, and the tree yielding fruit, whose seed was in itself, after his kind: and God saw that it was good.   In other words, God uniquely made us to do a specific function and it is deposited like a seed in you in which he created you to become.   You were not designed to do what another person is doing because he formed you with a specific assignment. 2 Peter 1:10-11 says, "Wherefore the rather, bretheren, give diligence to make *your calling* and election sure: for if ye do these things, you shall never fall: (vs 11), For so an entrance shall be ministered unto you abundantly into the everlasting kingdom of our Lord and Savior Jesus Christ. We must understand scripture and not mans theology, feelings or opinions. For those who dare to violate scripture, the penalty will end up teaching error to His Church. Romans 11:29 says, "For the gifts and calling of God are without repentance. We can view this as our Creator placing a variety of gifts in us and a specific calling in which we were made to become.   In the bible says Psalms 21:8, "Thine hand shall find out all thine enemies, thy right hand shall find out those that hate thee. Benjamin, a descendant from the Tribe of Benjamin, name has been defined as "Son of My Right Hand". The illustration does not imply to a single person but to a communion, network or body of people who have been called out of darkness to be a source of light and truth in righteous judgment to the body of Christ. The bible says in Psalm 111:7, "The works of His hands are verity and judgment. Clearly we see that God has two hands, one of verity and one of judgment. The word "Verify" in Hebrew is the word for TRUTH. With one hand, God brings forth truth and with the other hand, he brings forth judgment. God is moving to bring us into harmony with truth. What a beautiful coordination in all the works of his Hands?

Every time God releases a new dimension of His purpose he then brings a measure needed to bring us into alignment with that purpose. If he can do this through a positive initiation, he will do also in dealings of His right hand. But if corrective measures are needed, God will stretch forth his left hand and bring negative forces into action of teach us a particular lesson. There are times we pray for God to stretch for his right hand of verity, because we are hungry for a blessing and truth, which he graciously conveys to us in His Word.

In Isaiah 54:16-17 the Bible says, "Behold, I have created the smith that bloweth the coals of fire, and that bringeth forth an instrument for his work; and I have created the waster to destroyer." A typical response would be to disseminate that God created evil. The bible is clear that God had to create evil with good so that his creation could make a choice. Isaiah 45:7 states, "That they may know from the rising of the sun, and from the west that there is none beside me. I am the Lord and there is none else. I formed the light and darkness. I make peace and create evil. I the lord do all these things." Thus, the epitome of Gods ability and power should never be questioned. Every person God created has this innate ability to realize that the creator of all creation is omnipotent (all powerful).

However, the mind of mankind attempts to question his authority without the ability to comprehend. The continuous notion of the creation operating in unbelief is mind blowing. The same pattern continues to flourish as new pastor's implement initiatives with a different intention which results practicing the same patterns of their former leaders. The problem lies in the fact that they expect a different outcome. This is the acute and accurate definition of insanity unless the Church can identify and plug into the true source of power, God have mercy on mankind's soul.

It is so apparent that the creature of the creator has been hoodwinked with these doctrine of devils. It appears that the doubters of the true living God have no fear of the wrath of God. Proverbs 6:27 says, "Can a man take fire in his bosom, and his clothes not be burned?" The enemy has been casted to dwell in outer darkness and he continues to disguise truth with evil in order to draw others into eternal damnation. Deception has continued to plague the body of Christ within the advent of understanding the calling of God with respect to the hand of God. As we examine the hand of God, we can see that our physical makeup is parallel to his very image. The same sentiments are parallel to God with the image of his body or what we have construed to be the Church. The body of Christ has also been coaxed into a mindset of overlapping the unique gifts illustrated. The bible says in Ephesians 4:11, and he gave some first the Apostles, Prophets, Evangelists, Pastors and Teachers. It appears throughout the discourse of Church development, the

Pastor was placed in charge. Who said, the pastor was in charge? The truth of the matter will solely be determined as the individual who carries the vision of the Lord.

Many will take the reference given in the 23 Chapter of Jeremiah that he would give shepherds after his own heart. Listen beloved, all five function play the part in shepherding the flock. Just because one of the five gifts is called the pastor does not mean the pastor is in charge. A pastor has a responsibility just like the other four gifts mentioned have responsibility. Many theologians have tried to nullify the other fivefold gifts and try merge them into four. We are made in his likeness so that alone would nullify this philosophical assumption. It appears that many don't want to give credence to the office of teacher because of the use of "and" in scripture. This is merely a gesture of man attempting to take away the significance of the office of the teacher. Although the office of the Pastor is apt to teach, there is no proof whatsoever that he is a teacher. The foolishness of man in their attempt to equate one with a Shepherds anointing with on who carries the mark of a Shepherd. This is just another effort to change the plan illustrated by God in reference to His hand. This effort also attempts to assimilate a model Church under the same pattern as a Shepherd in a pasture which conveys the erroneous concept of Church leadership. Because God is a pattern driven creator and sustainer of our soul, we must understand His plan over our own. The Church has not fulfilled its efforts primarily because it has become delusional in its efforts.

The Word of God should always be our primary source for direction unless the spirit of God has intervened. It is a normal directive for the Holy Spirit to intervene and fulfill the mission at hand. The hand of God is uniquely designed to facilitate the plan and will of God. In other words, God has given us a blue print for a *Rolls Royce* but the Church continues to build a volts wagon design and mentality. The precedent here in referencing a car is not intended to minimize the significance of what God intended for the Church but rather to indicate the value of the Rolls Royce versus a volts wagon, a tremendous difference. The creature has chosen to do its own plan and design instead of understanding and implementing the design in origination. There are millions of Christians who do not believe that God created everything. In essence, God created evil but he himself is not evil. They prefer to believe as the worlds system has taught them that God created good, and the devil created evil.

Isaiah 45:7 states, "That they may know from the rising of the sun, and from the west, that there is none beside me. I am the Lord, and there is none else. I form the light and created darkness I make peace and created evil. I the Lord do all these things." But let us understand! The good that God uses comes from God. The evil that God uses is created by God only for the purpose that he has for it. The Bible states that God is good, is life, is light. Nowhere does the Bible say that God is evil. But, the bible does declare that God created evil. There is a vast difference because evil had to be present for God to give his creation the choice between good and evil. This would better illustrate the free will moral agent that God had created in each of us to characterize a choice. Anything that is absolutely eternal is not only unending, but is also unchangeable.

Anything that changes in any way is not eternal, for in the change some characteristics are left behind and a new one is acquired. In every change something ends and something else begins, at least in form. That which dwells in an eternal state knows no change. Change is possible only in that which is limited, imperfect or not fully developed. The Lord declares to himself in Malachi 3:6, "I am the Lord, I Change not. Apostle James declares in

James 1:17, "with whom there is no Variableness, neither shadow of turning". But we, in our spiritual discourse, are still being changed! "And all of us... are constantly being transfigured into His very own image in ever increasing splendor and from one degree of glory to another.

The life of God that has been deposited in us, which is His Word, is perfect and will never change. The manifestation of that life, however, is subjected to a process limited by our understanding of His Word. As we delve further, we find no evidence that the present paradigm of the Church is neither relevant nor accurate. Whoever said the Pastor was in charge? As we look at the association of Jesus Christ being the Good Shepherd, it is apparent that the majority of Churches have chosen foolishly to omit or downplay other viable functions that are relevant to fulfill the mandate of the great commission.

As we look at the current demise of function alignment, it is quite clear that the Church substructure is missing key ingredients that would allow the Church to be wholesome and viable. Needless to say, the Church has fallen prey to humanism and opinions of people who have fallen prey to their own intelligence. Instead of plugging in, these theologians with brilliant mind's have forsaken the cardinal sin of self indulgence in their own intellect. Moreover, the Church is deformed and will continue to operate as handicapped until the body of Christ discovers the essentials of all five functions present and relevant in their disposition. And, until the body of Christ discover each function has a vital role to play in the culmination to the Church being perfected and the manifestation of the sons of God. When the gifts are fully functioning in the Church with the hand of God present, the true essence of God's grace shall be displayed and implemented for the sole purpose of the power of God being released in an un-measureable precedence.

Chapter 6:

The Need to Plug Into the Blueprint

Place us back in your hands father on your Potter's wheel so that the body of Christ can be in Kingdom Alignment. The original plan of God was to have man at the helm leading us into the promise land. Nevertheless, mankind was given the responsibility to spread Gospel to every nation, kindred and tongue. Everyone has a role to play in the dissemination of the word of God. The number six has a significant association with a reference to man. However, if you take the same number six and add two more sixes to make it three digits, you have the number for Satan. It is amazing to see how the enemy will attempt to duplicate and mimic God's creative ability.

The bible says in Job 14:1, "Man that is born of woman is of few days, and full of trouble. Considering this nature of humanity, it is clear that man has had trouble on his hand from the beginning making it apparent man does not function in proper authority without having an intimate relationship with God. It is clear where man tries to share authority as the copilot when in essence God is the pilot over every believers life. This same pattern of shared authority is prevalent with male and female. Rather than working together, there seems to be feud set for competition. God never intended for both male and female to compete against one another. But, God did set prescribed guidelines for the role of women and men. Furthermore, God instructed the male to be head of the household. In other words, the male serving as the husband takes on the lead role in the home. The female serving as the wife becomes the help meet often confused with help mate. Additionally speaking, both male and female are needed to make sure the Church is brought into alignment with the plan and will of God. Within every seasonal stanza of time, man and woman have gone through a discourse of role reversal.

This is not suggesting that God made any changes with the original design. The enemy has created havoc and launched an endless battle on the institution of marriage especially marriages inside of the Church. Due to the advent of sin and the affects sin conveys on marriages the devil has made efforts to deter the Church from walking in its full authority. Considering this, we can do longer adapt to old patterns of religion which exclude the aid of the Holy Spirit and must understand the power of duplication or reproduction.

God is so profound in how he disseminates his power through his word. He has the uncanny ability to relay profound nuggets of wisdom through the portal of revelation. Unfortunately, man has a strong tendency to abdicate from the precious benefits of righteousness given man's quest and yearning to be right, in sense of intellectual stimulation. Man has continuously struggled with the endeavor to think without the participation of the Holy Spirit. Consequently, man's quest for pre-eminence has continued to propel mankind to be further away from experiencing the full measure of holiness and righteousness. The natural mind does not comprehend the significance and intent of spiritual concepts which continue to baffle mankind. Something as simple as a seed reproduced after its own kind has caused a spinoff in the laws of reproduction. Reproduction is best illustrated with the process of seed time and harvest. Can an orange reproduce an apple or can a peach produce a grape. The Church's seeding process has been contaminated with the opinions of mankind. The demise of holiness and righteousness is contingent on the Church reconnecting to the spirit of God. The tenacity of leaders who feel they can operate in multiple callings or functions has created a new breed in the Church. The invasion of a schizophrenic spirit has been embarked on the Church. Schizophrenia is a term is used in the medical community to define a person with a psychotic disorder characterized by loss of contact with the environment, noticeable deterioration in the level of function in everyday life, and by disintegration of personality expressed as a disorder of feeling, thought and conduct. This disorder, as it relates to the out of alignment perspective, characterizes that a person may have dual or multiple personalities. Another common term manic depression (more up-to-date term is bipolar) deals with mood swings. There is a battle going on with the Church as it battles to coexist. That is, the religious side wants to over-ride the spiritual side. As a writer, I have a responsibility to make sure that we are not maligning the integrity of the conditions or the medical community. The terms are utilized as a comparison to promulgate the serious problem that has invaded the Church and serves as a classical example of crop failure. Everyone can appreciate a farmer for planting more than one type of seed in his garden. The problem with crop failure or the failure of a double-minded man has some common tendencies. Each requires the environment to play an essential role in the process. When the environment fails, neither crop or the person suffering from any of these disorders can be effective. While authenticity is a validation from heaven, God gave a detailed blue print as to how he wanted his gifts to be illustrated. We can see the simplicity of the concept carries greater weight in the spirit of reproduction when viewed from seed time and harvest perspective. In other words, seeds can only be reproduced by the same type of seed you desire to produce. The same principle applies in the Church. God has provided a significant illustration in how gifts are to be reproduced by someone who has same gifting which begs the question: If an orange is incapable of reproducing an apple or peach reproducing a grape, how do you explain pastors trying to produce prophets, evangelist trying to produce teachers and prophets trying to produce apostles. Neither efforts can possibly be effective or relevant. While it is plausible to compare an orange being squeezed as comparing to the anointing, the juice is a fragrance from the orange itself, as the anointing is from God.

It is true that believers may be called to one function but flow in different anointing. Every believer is entitled to flow in the anointing but it is contingent of their level of faith. Some have a hard time trying to distinguish the difference. While it is plausible to compare an orange being squeezed as comparable to the anointing, the juice is a fragrance from the orange itself as the anointing is from God. Due to the plausibility of a fruitless outcome, many inside the Church violate these very pertinent principles that were designed to foster a reproduction system sent from heaven. God's plans were geared towards gift reassignment to prepare future generations with gifts after its own kind. "God has ordered that every seed shall bring forth fruit after its own kind" (Genesis 1:11). Gods law of reproduction applies to the kingdom, to humans and to the spirit kingdom as well. Without fail, when a seed is planted in a plot of land, it produces a new plant identical to the plant from which the seed came. In other words, the apple does not fall too far from the tree. This expression of scripture illustrates that whatever your gift is that it does not fall too far from the source of the gift. This is clear evidence that the Church' present pattern has deviated from the plan and will of God. The concept obedience is better than a sacrifice is a direct shot at hitting the bull's eye. Relatively Speaking, any deviation is clearly a sacrifice for opinion rather than obedience to the truth. The Church, in its present condition, continues to spurn out of control due to the impotence and the lack of structure which is needed to take the Church into the 21st Century.

The key is effectiveness and efficiency. The Church has only embraced the Pastor as one of five components. Yet, it is essential that the Church understand the necessity for all functions to be in place. God's blue print has been written but not implemented. The Church has compromised its authority in the same likeness of the spirit of Jezebel. The spirit of error and the spirit of truth have coexisted since the eons of time. There is a diabolical plot for some men to be passive and their counter parts take on the spirit of Jezebel. This spirit is one where the man is suppose to be the head and the woman is suppose to be the follower of her husband. Since a Jezebel spirit counterfeits the prophetic anointing in gifts, calling and authority, a leader that serves the office of prophet will become a target of a Jezebel attack. A Prophetic Church (one that embraces the mantle of the prophet) and its prophetic leaders must realize that if the spirit of Elijah is going to return, so will its counter-spirit-the Jezebel spirit. Jesus warned the Church at Thyatira about this diabolical spirit called Jezebel. According to Revelation 19:10," Jezebel's aim is to silence God's prophets because it would destroy the testimony of Jesus Christ, which is the spirit of prophecy" It takes you away from the truth and from the words of our Lord given to us for the benefit of the Church, to follow what does not come from God. The premise behind this notion is to lure many faithful to God away from the real prophetic revelation that is given by God's grace. Let us clearly state, the Jezebel spirit is not geared only to women. Men have allowed this spirit to infiltrate them as well. There are men as well as women who have a quest for power, position and praise. We must understand the spirit is only named after Jezebel so we will only promulgate a history of Queen Jezebel or King Ahab. Most deceiving to many is that Jezebel was religious at best and did religious things. She was a daughter of Ethbaal, meaning "with Baal". She converted her husband King Ahab to follow baal. Ahab married her against God's command. The name Jezebel specifically means "without dwelling or habitation."

A true explanation of Jezebel can clearly be described as the worship of self-will, the clear battle with jezebel spirit is over people. In the Church, the spirit of jezebel desires to rule and control the people of God. She is a supporter of, and heavily influential in, religious organization as well as politics. While Jezebel is religious, she wields her false power against the true prophetic flow and prophets of God. Specifically, she hates repentance, humility, and intercessory prayer, because each destroy her strongholds of stubbornness and pride. Jezebel loves to protect the pseudo power they really don't have. It is based on intimidation in order to cloud the minds of those they desire to oppress. Intimidation is just one way the spirit of Jezebel seeks to move the person through threats. This use of fear subsequently and subsequently losing something as a result, puts the victim under control of the jezebel spirit. This is a form of black mail and so far from God's love. Fear for control and blackmail are improper channels, use of illegitimate power and authority, projection of power that is not ours to use. By no means does this insinuate that a person should not stand up for himself, but rather it should be done through proper channels.

Manipulating, intimidating and dominating another human being is blatant misuse of control and illegitimate authority. The first and most important aspect of all shipwrecks is inexperience followed by lack of accountability. This could be the result of conditions that are deemed acts of God. Preachers, from all walks of life seem to become independent that they run their ministries without any checks and balances. Therefore, more preachers are abandoning a need to have spiritual parents or a board to give accountability. As the Church progresses into a new dimension the way the Churches are run has opened a flood gate of inquiry because the way finances are being used has brought needed exposure. As a result, we have countless cases where embezzlement and countless of other infraction have come to an all time high. Integrity and sexual misconduct has always hung around the Church. The Church is run into a brick wall of leaders who have caused the Church to improperly record finances and has prompted further investigation.

Many of our leaders are guilty of poor record keeping and countless attempts to hide money that has never been recorded in their books. The free for all degradation has placed the Church under scrutiny that would not be the case if proper checks and balances were implemented. It appears that many of these religious entities operate with a mindset that prompts the IRS to catch them if they can. This attitude is that we are not that significant to warrant attention of the Internal Revenue Services.   In all of the devious acts, the organization relies on old organizational guidelines that have been out of date.   Furthermore, these organizations are not keeping up with up-to-date practices that would put them in compliance with IRS.   For instance, the Church conducts a week long revival in which an agreement has been set in place in which the speaker would get 50% and the Church would get 50%. At the end of the revival, the Church would keep all the checks and hand an envelope with half of everything that came in as part of the offerings. Once the Church or Church leader has handed the money to the speaker, he or the Church has committed a criminal offense. The Church should never hand over cash. Any outlay of cash should be dispersed in a check. This is just one of many areas that the Church needs to improve for accountability purposes and IRS compliance.

Chapter 7:

The Removal of Religious Cows

The foundation of Church is pure and sure because Jesus Christ is the Chief Corner Stone. This foundation shall not be cracked nor can it be penetrated. Needless to say, the house of the Lord is where we must begin to clean up in order to bring about a change that will ultimately enhance the life of the Church for the greater good. 1 Peter 4:17 says, "For the time is come that judgment must begin at the house of God: and if it first begin at us, what shall the end be of them that obey not the gospel of God?" There is a strong hold on the Church where independence and lack of accountability is apparent revealing the abdication of Spiritual Parents and Church Mothers to the point of non existence. I Timothy 3:15 states: "But if I tarry long, that thou mayest know how thou oughtest to be have thyself in the house of God, which is the Church of the living God, the pillar and ground of the truth. The responsibility of being a set leader of God's flock is a "good work" which should not be taken lightly. I Timothy 3:1-7 states, "This is a true saying, if a man desire the office of a bishop, he desireth a good work. A bishop then must be blameless, the husband of one wife, vigilant, sober, of good behavior, given to hospitality, apt to teach; Not given to wine, no striker, not greedy of filthy lucre; but patient, not a brawler, not covetous; One that ruleth well his own house, having his children in subjection with gravity; (For if a man know not how to rule his own house, how shall he take care of the Church of God?)

Not a novice, lest being lifted up with pride he fall into the condemnation of the devil. Moreover he must have a good report of them which are without; lest he fall into reproach and the snare of the devil. In Acts 20:28, Paul warned the leaders in Ephesus to "Take heed therefore to yourselves" Preachers must understand that their depraved heart is capable of all sorts of vile sins and they are not immune to committing the vilest of sins. Furthermore, it is the Churches that are "the pillar and ground of the truth" whom God "hath purchased with his own blood, the Churches need to be warned. The spiritual leader has been entrusted with the sacred oversight of Gods people! It appears however that there is a new breed of leaders who operate with the mentality that no one can sit them down because God is the one to put them in the position. These new preachers have an array of dirty linen in their own house in need of cleansing.

For those who keep their mouth shut in an attempt to mind their own business, become accomplices in the sin. Instead of covering up the sin, attempts should be made to help our brother or sister to be an overcomer. Sadly, it is not a new thing to hear a spiritual leader loving the sins of the world more than loving Christ. Although adultery is an ungodly and should be abhorred and avoided, it is apparent that one would rather be in an affair with a woman than a man. Both of these choices are ungodly and should be avoided at all cost. We can look at it this way marriage is a commitment between a man and a woman. There is no room for anyone else to be apart of this institution. Each spouse must be faithful to your mate or find one and be faithful is the only option. It is unimaginable to comprehend men lusting one toward another man or a woman lusting after another woman.

Yet, with the advent of the down low brothers the act of sodomy has come to the forefront. It is unimaginable to comprehend men lusting one toward another. Contrary to popular beliefs, men have been put in positions by human boards who appoint them based on human factors such as degrees, preaching ability and a host of other subjective factors held by board members. Preachers falling into sin is not new but is why sodomy is occurring among so many preachers today. We do know Paul spoke prophetically saying, "This know also, that in the last days perilous times shall come. For men shall be lovers of their own selves..."2Timothy 3:1,2. The vilest of sin! Just the thought of a man performing the "unseemly" act of sodomy is repulsive and to think a preacher of the Gospel participating in such is most nauseating! These men are deceivers! They are living a lie!

When they stand behind the sacred pulpit and open the bible, they were living a lie! This deeply rooted act of abomination has crept into our Churches and pulpits prompting other men who will use their position to continue this diabolical deed. The bible speaks of this behavior as an abomination. The word abomination in its own rite gives off the impression of a detestable act that is far greater than just sin. Spiritual acumen or sensitivity to the spiritual ream is often the missing element created by denominational alliances, theology and ideologies. Considering this, the Carnal Church is likened to a spineless organization because the spiritual leader is subject to the deacon board or board of trustees. How do preachers preach the very word of God with no discernment, not realization, no conviction, no guilt that God is supposed to be speaking through them as well as to those under the sound of their voice? It is due to the fact that some of these preachers are no more than seminary graduates without spiritual maturity. What does this mean? Simply, many are called and few are chosen. For the religious, the term" chosen" is deeply seated ink pulpit committees, pastoral recruitment committees have been given the responsibility to find a replacement for the vacancies in their house.

This is a classic example of the flock choosing the leader instead of God selecting the leader for them. This democratic selection process is an ungodly in that it gives the people authority to choose what God alone can appoint. Given the prevalence of this process, the Church has opened a gateway for preachers who are detached from the people to come in with their own agendas are to release their homophobic beliefs among the Church. Are these preachers so self-confident to think God's word is for others but not for themselves? For instance, do these men believe that 1 Corinthians 6:9-10: " Know ye not that the unrighteous shall not inherit the kingdom of God? Be not deceived; neither fornicators, nor idolaters, nor adulterers, nor effeminate, nor abusers of themselves with mankind, nor thieves, nor covetous, nor drunkards, nor revilers, nor extortionist, shall inherit the kingdom of God," was pertinent to all others but them? They undoubtedly forget Galatians 6:7" Be not deceived, God is not mocked: for whatsoever a man soweth, that shall he also reap."   A man lying with another man is defilement so says God! God does not want his children in sin or the sin of Sodomy. It is clear the residue of sin of sodomy still exist in our Churches today. As in the days of Noah and Ham, God is watching the sin of Sodom grow so grievous to the God of Heaven and earth the time of judgment was about to arrive. So is it with all of us, sin will be judged. Proverbs 9:17, says, "Stolen waters are sweet, and bread eaten in secret is pleasant. The prohibition of Sodomy, as with any sin, makes itself most appealing to the fallen nature. These preacher participating in these lewd acts thought they were getting away with it according to proverbs 5:21.......but" .... The ways of man are before the eyes of the LORD, and he pondereth all his going." The first reference to Sodom was Genesis 10:19 and the second reference to Sodom is Genesis 13:10. Here we are told " Lot lifted up his eyes, and behold all the plain of Jordan, that it was well watered every where, before the Lord destroyed Sodom and Gomorrah, even as the garden of the Lord, like the land of Egypt, as thou comest out unto Zoar." The sins of Sodom would be known fact to both Abram and Lot. It may be sure that Lot had often looked out of his tent at the well watered "pain of the Jordan". He could see the amazing potential in living there in spite of the sins of the inhabitants. It is apparent that the Church leaders today that are caught up in their sins have no regard for their members. Rather, these leaders prey on a sect of members who may display traits of candidacy of a life of sodomy. Now they can view this stretch of imagination never cease to amaze me. The victims who may or may not realize the hypocrisy of participating with their spiritual leader because they see him play a role with them. Needless to say, these victim seem to think and act like Lot and his wife as a type of today's Christian can be seen. All was fine as long as Lot walked with Abram, who was walking with God.

Many look fine as they walk with others in the Church building. They shake hands, they tithe, they participate in many of the activities, and often they occupy the place of leadership. In the Lot family, it may have been mentioned there is ministry potential in that couple. As long as Lot and his wife walked with Abram, they were doing fine. The decision, an expensive one by any means, came in regard to the financial loss that Lot and his wife would loose by leaving Sodom and Gomorrah. This decision held detrimental consequences for Lot and his family. When the time was at hand, Lot's heart had already decided. Lot's fall and failure happened suddenly in the physical appearance it was in process over a period of time.

Lot looked with the physical eye and not the spiritual eye of faith. Lots decision was made based on the advice from the deep recesses of his heart. Looking out on the plains before him and making this decision by sight led to his earthly walk separate and opposite from Abram. The same method of reasoning led him and his family down into Sodom. So much continues to rest upon the daily decision preachers make in their life. The bible says in Job

31:1, " I made a covenant with mine eyes...." When Lot left Abram he didn't rush headlong down to Sodom but scripture states he dwelled in the cities of the plain and pitched his tent toward Sodom." Lot eventually moved into Sodom and stayed there for some time. However, one day Lot and his family were taken into captivity by "Amraphel King of Shinar, Arioch King of Ellasar, Chedorlaomer King of Elam, and Tidal King of Nations." Lots life had taken another turn. But fortunately Lot's captivity came to an end when he and his family were rescued by his uncle, Abram. Was this a wake up call to Lot? In accordance to 1 Corinthians 15:34, "Awake to righteousness, and sin not...." During the rescue attempt by Abram, he was offered a reward from Sodom's King but being a man of God Abram told the King of Sodom he would not "take anything that is thine." All the counterfeit professing Christian preachers and members will be overtaken by the wrath to come on this earth but all the just the "Lots" will be delivered.

Chapter 8:

The Eradication of Cosmetic Christianity

The purpose of the Church is to display the character of Christ and restore the lost through the process of salvation. Putting on the image of God should be the true endeavor of every Christian. Can we truly say that his character resides in everyone who claims to be a Christian. How many Christians are truly operating with a face of a clown? Make up, camouflage, veil, and coverings are only devices used to shield us from those looking in. However, make-up is a useful cosmetic resource used to accentuate a woman in a complementary manner of her appearance. Our reference here to cosmetics has nothing to do with the reference to Christianity.

Although, the wearing of mask could have similar effects. The expression in terms of Christianity is primarily to shield us from revealing ones true self. There is a difference from a believer who hides themselves in Christ Jesus and those who pretend to be Christians for other motives. The Church has always existed with the wheat and the tare. Can we truly say that the enemy dwells in the Church or that he drops by for a visit? Nevertheless, it appears the disposition or posture of the real Church is dressed up with finest cloths, wears a weak facial foundation of foolishness and pretention on their face. It appears to be made up with bright red lipstick resembling the bride of Frankenstein rather than the bride of Christ.

The predisposition is that we continue to allow the patterns of convenience to serve as the blue print of the divine Church that God called the ecclesia. The intent of the Church purposed to bring individuals out of darkness into the marvelous light. But, can we truly walk in the light without dipping back into darkness? What causes the tendency of those called out of darkness to run back into the pit of darkness. It is true in a superficial disposition that the Church realistic through the religious rhetoric and lack of spiritual enlightenment. The cosmetic

82

concept of Church is truly superficial because we allow everyone to claim themselves as a member of the Church. In addition, there are those who claim to be members of a Church just because their name is on the roster.

From such groups as Wicca to overt groups like that of Satanist, there is an array of counterfeit groups who hide behind the banner of Christianity. While each group may have a religious base, there is no evidence of the spirit of Christ within these organizations, as they operate with a spirit of the devil. Each organization uses Christianity to lure in the lukewarm or even those who may not have a strong foundation. The premise here is to lure them from the foundation of truth and infuse concepts contrary to the word of God. Deception has grown to an all time high with its intent to function with a disguised truth. But, the deception shall be revealed as the deceiver operating in the spirit of error. This is one of the most frightening deception's because the enemy has brought such confusion and doubt that many believers fall prey to these diabolical plots.

The Apostle Paul cautioned the Corinthians on this: "Be honest in your estimate of yourselves, it is important that you don't misinterpret yourselves as people." Certainly the problem was addressed in the book of

Revelation when the seven Churches of Asia had a plumb line of measurement dropped into their midst by God himself. They all thought themselves to be something they were not. Only one of them measured up. Thus, we must understand that God used the plumb line as a measuring tool to indicate that six of the seven did not measure up. How does today's Church measure up to the same standard as the one that did meet God's criteria?

It is absurd to believe that the present disposition of the Church is in direct alignment with the will and purpose of God. The cosmetic veil has hindered the Church from moving out of the distorted state that it is a representation of the false and powerless Church. And, the Church can't comprehend the difference between the spirit of truth and the spirit of error. In 2 Corinthians 6:14 , the bible says, " Be ye not unequally yoked together with unbelievers: for what fellowship hath righteousness with unrighteousness? And what communion hath light with darkness? In other words, the present Church is only enamored with the education and the, credentials of their Spiritual Leader, and his ability to move a crowd of people. The bible says in Matthew 23:16-22 "Woe unto you, ye blind guides, which say, whosoever shall swear by ; but the temple, it is nothing; but whosoever shall swear

84

by the gold of the temple he is a debtor! Ye fools and blind guides: for whether is greater, the gold, or the temple that sanctifieth the gold?   And, Whosoever shall swear by the altar, it is nothing; but whosoever sweareth by the gift that is upon it, he is guilty.   Ye fools and blind: for whether is greater, the gift, or the altar that sanctified the gift? Whoso therefore shall swear by the altar sweareth by it, and by all things theron. And whoso shall swear by the temple, sweareth by it, and by him that dwelleth therein. An he that shall swear by heaven, sweareth by the throne of God, and by him that sitteth thereon. It appears that many will address God in the form of the letter of the law but not fully understand the spiritual access by way of embracing the mind of God through the spiritual access of Jesus Christ. Many choose to follow those that teach the law, but don't have the mind of God. We have approached a time where many will fall away from the faith. I Timothy 4:1, " Now the Spirit speaketh expressly, that in the latter times some shall depart from the faith, giving heed to seducing spirits, and doctrines of devils" Presently, the Church is dealing with a great fall away. Many have embraced new form of grace from an erroneous concept where they have departed from the Church. They are feeling that they don't need the Church anymore, and they would rather sit at home and do their own thing.

This is a very dangerous initiative of the New World Order for which it is causing believers to think that they don't need to be in the Church to be saved. Unfortunately, they claimed to have taken the scriptures out of context of justification in order to substantiate their feud with the Church and it's hierarchy. While there are serious problems in the Church, there is no justification for members of the body of Christ to stay home unless they are sick and shut in. In other words, they are incapable of getting to the Church because of medical reasons. Some people will use this as a manipulative way to justify that they are just sick of the mess that occurs in the Church. Unfortunately, the efforts to clean up the mess will only occur when the true Church stands up and walk in the power of the word of God. The enemy has launched his efforts to hinder the progress of the Church through deceitful efforts that hinder people from following the will of God. However, good always outweighs evil and its efforts to draw believers away from the faith, and to abort the plans and will of God.

The Church must stand up in the splendor of Righteousness and Holiness. It is time for the Church to abdicate from human efforts and embrace the authority of the Word of God and the power that is connected with it. We must unite to thwarts the devils efforts to divide and conquer. However, he has already deceived himself to think that we shall stand by and do nothing. Because of the attacks that have been levied on the Church, there are many reports of Pastor coming forth and declaring anonymously that they only have the position as a means to take care of their family. A constituents had the audacity to say that he preaches the gospel but , he does not believe in the God of the gospel. The dispelling notion here is this individual had been appointed over a flock of God that does not know what their leader believes. This is a new pattern illustrating the blind leading the blind. What are the effects of a non-believing leader who pretends to believe? This is a dangerous person who has developed the ability to preach the gospel, but he does not believe in the gospel he preaches. This type person poses a major threat to the Kingdom because they foster an atmosphere or platform for the devil to teach the doctrine of devils. The pit of hell would be filled with suckers who believed in their demonic agenda to pull down and destroy the works of God! In truth, the blood bought Church of God can't be destroyed by the enemy.

This is one mission that is impossible. As we stated in Matthew 11:12, "And From the days of John the Baptist until now the Kingdom of Heaven suffers violence, and violent men take it by force." When one reads the above mentioned text, they literally believe by comprehending that the enemy can take anything away from God. In reality, the believers yield their kingdom authority by not being at their post, in the word or at the right Church. Each believer is given an assignment that is a door way to purpose and destiny. The enemy has tricked many believers into yielding their authority because he is empowered by their lack of faith.

The enemy continues gaining stride in the race when a believer abandons their position of authority. Although the devil is a spirit, he is not omnipotent. He can only get access to strength from the believers who give their authority to the enemy. To maintain and sustain strength believers must gain access to knowledge of through the mind of God by a spiritual biblical cord. However, we must continue to read, study and meditate on the word of God. This will enable the believer to plug into the mind of God and cause his power to be released into the believer. As each believer increases their level of faith, the opportunity to walk in a new dimension of God is given and the believer receives "access granted" when utilizing the access key.

There are many Christians pretending to be connected, but there are not walking in the maturity or the authority that has been made available. In acts 19:14, the Seven Sons of Sceva and the vagabond Jews have witness the Spiritual authority of Jesus Christ. The Sons of Sceva tried to imitate the authority of Christ while attempting to cast out a devil. However, the demon's said Jesus I know and Paul I know but who are you. This is a message to those pretending to operate under the anointing: You are in a very dangerous position. The demon did recognize the person trying to imitate Jesus Christ or Paul and responded in an adversarial manner and then beat the cloths off of the vagabond Jews and causing an uproar never seen before. Demons have power but they are not all powerful. When a believer's stands up and embraces the power that God has entitled them to operate in, the body of Christ becomes empowered to shut down the enemy's points of access. The Church and the inhabitants of the Church have been given keys to the Kingdom. However, the Church has been a distracted by the enemy causing the key hole and the lock to be off alignment with keys of authority.

The keys of authority are granted only to all persons who walk in the light of God. We are truly in perilous times when the enemy tries to manifest as a light bearer. Furthermore, it is more important that believers learn how to take the mask (cosmetic) off and walk in their divine authority. This authority will grant them access to a deeper dimension in God. The hand of God provides keys that will enable the believers to function in his authority.

Chapter 9:
Stolen Femininity Through Identity Theft

As we look through the portals of time, we find that woman have been under an enormous amount of atrocity and a great amount of scrutiny. It also appears that women have had to play a multitude of the roles in the girlfriend, prostitute, wife, concubine, the lesbian lover, the other woman and whatever the role to get the job done. Needless to say, the plight for women perhaps could be construed as a journey from hell and back. While the discourse may have required them to clean houses, scrub floors and serve as an occasional sex toy to make ends meet, this does not discredit all the wonderful attributes that women had to overcome to rescue their children from a life obscurity.

The psychological damage has played a tremendous role in the plight of some of the greatest women in the word. Even during the early stages of life, little girls and

91

boys spend a great deal of time playing together. It is during this stage when the children begin to notice the differences in body development. The body composition begins to change and the inquisitive nature of the children find a need explore the differences of their body development. It is a tremendous need for parents to be extremely watchful over the welfare of their children. In order to expand and secure a greater level of growth for their children, parents must raise their level of consciousness regarding demonic doorways.

It was also essential that parents needed to scrutinize who & where their children sleep on extended stays or overnight sleep over's. The doorway to demonic access have been cultivated and infiltrated during midnight hours. The enemy implemented its campaign while adults are sleeping. Unfortunately, many parents are unaware of these activities until they catch their children in the act. The assailant in this matter could be an older sibling, an uncle, an aunt or another distant relative. Each parent plays an important role in cultivating their children's legacy in life by spending quality time with them. When little boys do not get adequate time with their father, they tend to spend majority of their time in the female arena. The family structure is altered by the absentee farther and tends to cause the child suffer in terms of developing habits of a women. Because of the father's absence, the little boy misses the chance to be in his fathers presence. This action creates an adverse reaction to the building of the children's future development in the sexual identity. In other words, both parent need to bring a balanced approach for their children's over makeup.

The absentee father is a major part of the problem of little boys being emotionally dependent on his mother and begins to act like a little girl. Contrary, the same bonding requirements are needed for little girls who don't have a mother to help influence them. The need for little girls to bond with their mothers just as little boys need to bond with their father. The Tom Boy status is a prevalent spirit that has moved rampantly in our society. Little girls are developing unholy alliances that perpetuate sexual relationship with little girls at a very early age. This prevalent spirit is precipitated by a strong transference of a male domineering trait inside of a female. The children engaged in this behavior are attacked with severe peer pressure to go with the flow. This life changing decision carries grave medical effects that can severely damaged the normally development of the child. The parents, who are fearful of public shame, make the matters worse by placing the matter under the rug. The atrocity of this event compels medical physicians to attempt to change the mindset through efforts of mental assent. This methodological approach for this endeavor is to be controlled by an atmosphere where the candidate for a sex change must be conditioned to alter its mindset from the mindset in which they were born with. Some countries have further catered to demise of women in the most negligent way. The negative side effects of our society always made some type of sexual innuendo towards women from the days of slavery to board room.

The bull dagger mentality is an extremely domineering disposition that propel women to embrace and take the role as the strong stud of man in this lesbian relationship. The underling notion is that this person has illegally tried to be a man in terms of his role as Butch or Cedric. Needless to say, the act of pretending to be something in spite of the role reversal attempts is just a performance without an audience. Deception has tricked many to think that they can put on a costume of a man to become one. The plight for equality has propelled some to use sexual favors as an incentive for career advancement. The black widow is a predatory concept that fuels a seductive agenda for a bitter woman to lure a man into her web so that she can control him and ultimately kill him. The black widow carries the same diabolical tendencies as a python because the prey will literally end up lifeless. Each predator is a vehicle enabled to empower the woman to subdue her prey by squeezing the life out of them or by killing them as a symbol of their victory. Thus, the mandate of a predator is to violate the man either by emasculating his manhood or by squeezing the life out of the man in order to move to the next conquest.

Another version of a "Black Widow" is a kind of woman that lures men into their lives and marries them for their wealth. Once the relationship is on a solid foundation, she sets out a plan of action to kill her husband. The plan for wealth accumulation continues as the black widow sets out for her new victim as she changes her name with an alias and relocates to a new area. This plan is contingent on locating a wealthy candidate that is looking for a beautiful woman. Furthermore, she plays the hard to get type of woman and ends up reeling him into her web of death. As with all of her plans, she convinces him that she can't live without him and desire's to live the rest of her life with him. This spineless man falls into her trap as she convinces him that she will not be happy until they are married. This particular concept breeds a new derivative of an inferiority complex that keeps them bound.

The fact that women have not been placed in the forefront of the battlefield of warfare has caused many to feel useless outside of the house. However, men seem to think that it is their responsibility to prevent women from moving into the level and disposition that they were called. These legalistic Pharisee's have the audacity to speak on behalf of God to relegate women to step from behind the veil. Nevertheless, this false mindset forgets that God chooses the vessel to speak on his behalf as the Oracle of God. It is important to note here that a women speaking or preaching the word on behalf of God is not usurping her authority over man. Furthermore, it is time for men to understand that they are not the authority over the vessel God uses to speak or position as it pertains to His Church. There are too many souls headed to hell while men are concerned with who has the right to be in leadership. This is merely conjecture and it is so uneventful that God has to see this mess continue to be brewing. From the biblical days of Nimrod sleeping with his mother-in-law, there has been a great deal of moral decay in the world. Prostitution has also existed from the beginning of time. History continues to prove to be a valid source of reference. There is a conscious effort of women to supersede men in specific area of ministries that is causing great concern in our society. Jeremiah 31:22 says, "How long wilt though go about o though backsliding daughter? For the lord hath created a new thing in the earth. A woman shall compass a man. It is point where the body needs to have clear understanding. Many women read the word compass and assumed it means to surpass men.

However the word compass does not mean to surpass by any means. The word compass means to surround the man as in to secure a perimeter around him. In cases such as this, it serves a breeding ground for a great deal of disobedience and confusion. Some of the pearls of discomfort, stems from the decades of slavery. From a historical standpoint, black woman have been used extensively as sex toys by their slave owners. Many of the children have lost their identities because the slave owners refused to embrace them as their legitimate children. History has proved that many identities were stolen from their rightful legacy due to the shame and exposure of the slave owners. Although some of the children lived fruitful lives, their identity was stolen because of racial discrimination.

In effort of purporting mental cruelty, slave owners had the tendency to demoralize the men by making the husbands observe their wives being raped by the slave owners and their friends. The wives and daughters would take their own revenge and have casual sex with some of the slaves. The slave owners would receive an enormous amount of ridicule because they would later find that their wives and daughters were pregnant with babies from the slaves. In their eyes, it was extremely embarrassing before their friends & colleagues to rear a child that was created by one of their slaves. The shame of this nature would bring additional atrocity for the slave owners. In our present society,there are many women still feeling the sentiments of stones thrown at them from the days of slavery. In spite of the liberation from the slavery days, women are standing up boldly by trying to remove their head(husband) out of the way of the home and the Church to reposition him as a figure head. The cunning approach is very similar to the nature of the serpent who beguiled eve. This effect is now being labeled a man eating agenda which precipitated by an aggressive and domineering spirit. The anointing should never be used in such a competitive manner. This doorway is considered an access point that the enemy uses to create a competitive spirit between a man and woman. This competitive nature is spilled over into the institution of marriage. It appears that some wives refuse to submit to their head or any form of accountability. A new agenda has been birthed for women to skip over their headship and go straight to God directly.

This pattern of thinking is moving at such a rapid pace to fuel the birth of new ministries, Churches and fellowship. Women have launched an Ariel attack on men with the attempt to replace them. The competitive spirit is breeding ground of lustful desires for authority that is illegal and unauthorized for them to access. In other words, this spirit invades and tries to over-take the minds of women for the sincere efforts to posses authority not delegated by God or Man. There is another vile spirit that has invaded the body of Christ called the Leviathan. The bible says in Isaiah 27:1, "In that day the Lord with is sore and great and strong sword shall punish leviathan the piercing serpent, even leviathan the crooked serpent: and he shall slay the dragon that is in the sea." The lord uses an animal to depict the physical presence of Satan, which is an enemy to both God and mankind. Furthermore, this devil is describe in the spirit realm, likened to a extremely humongous crocodile that sneaks up on its prey, snatches it, takes it into the water and literally twists the life out it until it can then be consumed. In Isaiah, it is referred to as the "twisted serpent" having consumed its prey then flees. This demonstrates the vile nature of this spirit. Its influence is spread through those who are guilty of pride and self-righteous. Like the humongous crocodile this is a hidden spirit that can be lurking in the life of a Church, ready to strike when given the opportunity. When it is exposed for what it is, the leviathan looses it's hold over people as soon as they repent for coming under its influence.

The leviathan spirit is an extremely dangerous spirit that should not be played with nor is it one that you should be entered into lightly. This twisted spirit has made a covenant with many women due to their desire to have power and authority. This twisted spirit also encourages its counterparts to break covenant in friendships, in marriages and in Churches. The leviathan spirit encourages a victim to digress from accountability, commitment and all phases of authority. A *hermaphadite* is a person who has both male and female genitalia. However, there is great debate medical community that would rather call it intersex. This is considered a complex or undetermined issues of sexual development. In cases where confusion has set in, there are test done to do an analysis of chromosomes and hormones. Aside from this extreme case of sexual deviate, the spirit of incest has invaded our society. The same likeness has invaded the Church when the focus has been placed on a husband and wife being the head pastors. The spirit of a hermaphadite has spread into the Church for the mere pleasure of creating confusion. The misconception is premised on the notion that a husband and wife are one. The effort to become one in this context is an abuse on the person individuality. When God puts a couple together, there is a uniqueness because the two will complement one another. The mere effort of two people with the same identical calling creates another problem when it comes done to submission from other visiting leaders. This deviate behavior has transferred a multitude of spirits generationally damaging the internal makeup of the seeds produced. These seeds have fostered many severely tainted identities that have been stolen due to the negligence of wild sexual behavior.

Chapter 10:

The Historical Office of the Bishop

The historical Office of the Bishop is probably one of the most misunderstood functions in the body of Christ. Unlike any other office, it is not identical to a function where there is a specific calling. The Episcopal office of Bishop is not geared to a person because of a calling in the same light of the five fold governmental functions. Rather, the office is geared towards someone who is equipped to administrated or manage based on best practices to make the churches run smoothly, effectively and systematically. Traditionally speaking, the office of bishop normally reserved for males in the same light of the priesthood. This understanding is miffed by some leaders who are so busy trying to establish their own agenda or their own kingdom. Leaders of the previous generations grabbed hold of the office of Pastor and religiously abandoned the other four functions. Instead of pursuing a better understanding, they would rather deny the significance and purpose of each function. The fact of the matter, the ideology of the office of the bishopric, has no direct linkage with any of other the functions as well.

The role of the bishop is primarily an external administrative function through the gift of helps. Because of the misguided perception that the pastor is in charge(that is, unless he or she is the founder of the work of the church plant), a strong hold in connecting the pastor with this administrative appointment has been put in place. However, this notion would be better characterized as a typology of God creating Jesus Christ a little lower than angels. God saw fit to introduce Jesus Christ as the bishop of our souls and furthermore, modeled this reference after the angels because of the role angles play in the atmosphere and the hemisphere. What is the job description of an angel? The basic answer is to watch over the designated sphere for which the angels are assigned. The bishop's primary responsibilities are identical to the job description of the angels. No wonder God is so profound in his creative abilities. He created the office of Bishop to safeguard the grace of sacraments but also to exercise the delegated authority of the Apostles. Because of the delicacy of the function of the Apostle, it should be understood that Apostolic Succession is a Rite of Passage in terms of legitimacy.

In other words, the Apostles were given true legitimacy by Christ and they in return gave it to those who were granted the authority by imposition of hands. In other words, the hands of those who can trace their legitimacy by those who had hands laid onto them who were consecrated a bishop or affirmed as an Apostle. It is purely amazing that we don't see this particular pattern on the other four functions. We clearly see a reference to Samuel establishing a company of prophets but the pattern doesn't convey similar sentiments with regard to other gifts being reproduced with any level of succession. Though there is an implication that succession is implied with anyone who received their call from Christ, each function is authenticated by Jesus Christ because he is God and Humanity personified. After all, Jesus Christ was the delegator of every gift and the trainer for those who he conveyed the gift towards. It is imperative that the Church glean from Christ the importance of making sure every gift is reproduced after its own kind. The pattern for illustration purposes would be Jesus Christ training the initial 12 disciples who would become the foundational apostles. Despite the transitioning from Judas to Paul, there has been a tremendous pattern conveyed for the present day Church to follow. Each apostle was given the responsibilities to train up elders for the task of the New Testament Church.   This new testament pattern is the very act or responsibility of every leader to reproduce after its own kind. The law of nature is a very profound principle that God has put in place by act or deed.

According to Genesis 1:11-12: An God said, Let the earth bring forth grass, the herb yielding seed, and the fruit tree yielding fruit after his kind, whose see is in itself, upon the earth: and it was so......And the earth brought forth grass, and herb yielding seed after his kind, and the tree yielding fruit, whose seed was in itself, after his kind: and God saw that it was good. It is apparent that in this present day the ideology of the above mentioned scriptures which is so important is often overlooked and forgotten. The Church has failed to do what this scripture clearly indicates. The bible has given us an eternal blue print to walk in his divine authority and provisions. With that being said, the office of Bishop has been under great attack with those who only want the title but not the understanding of its purpose.   The bishop receives delegated authority from the lord to manage the work established by the hands of the apostle. So, it would be an erroneous assertion that bishops plant churches. Let us understand that delegated authority does not take the place of the duly called office of the Lord. Working outside your lane can be considered sin. This is a major problem in the church that some leaders are trying to do assignments that they were not authorized. Even though God made Jesus a little lower than angels, it was done for him because God is a pattern giver. While there are many prognosticators which believe that the bishops are apostles, the truth of the matter is man has fallen into just another delusion through theological assertion. We need to understand that a divine function and an appointed office are not one and the same.

The purpose of the office of Bishop is literally an external extension from the local Church serving in a managerial capacity that shall include other Churches in a particular fold. The bishop is known as the prince of the church.

A fold is a sphere of influence of Churches gathered under the administrative care of the bishop. While the apostle caries a charge to change the atmosphere, the imposition is he or she may go into areas untapped and pioneer a new Church plant. Once the work is planted,

107

new leadership is developed and the Church is self sustained, the apostle will head out to do the same task in another location. A key component is that the Apostle will be noted for establishing the work on the foundation of Jesus Christ and continue an existing relationship with the Church as a father figure. Now, this does not mean that a bishop can not be a spiritual father. The Church will be autonomous but will be relational rather than religious. There is a strong need for more relationship to occur in the body of Christ. When the true a living God is involved, their should be no inkling of racism. However, it is prevalent and still continues to exist. It is still lingering on both sides of the coin. There are some great kingdom minded churches on the majority side and some on the minority side. We need each other to serve the body to the fullest.

The widespread evolution of bishops has taken a negative turn because of alarming rate of men and women desiring to be known as great episcopates or for having large organization of episcopates. The office of Bishop has become an entrapment for men and women to obtain it by any means necessary. It appears that the office is for sale by some characters who not only don't have a true understanding but only desire to make money by selling the office with no relationship tied to it. The process of entering into episcopacy has further been mocked by some young men early in age who have no idea or have a minute idea of the intricate details. Furthermore, these young men are arrogant and do not desire to be trained. They only want the appearance and the title but do not desire to do the work required by the office. These same young men are eager to be in the position of presiding prelate after serving in the episcopacy for a couple of years. The attitude of these men and women are categorically atrocious because they have no patience to wait on the time and receive proper instructions before moving up in the next level of episcopacy. Because of the lack of knowledge and a desire to be mega in numbers, they begin to reproduce after their own kind. Thus, this negative light is indicative of a bad seed reproducing after its own kind.

The body of Christ has been tainted with young preachers who have poor work ethics, no value in the process, impatient in their purpose and no commitment the values of episcopacy. These individuals rather change the rules than follow them. Needless to say, the effect these young leaders have on our society and the Church is truly a damaging one at best. The effects of this notion propel a skewed perspective to younger preachers who have not paid the way with sweat equity. These young preachers entering into episcopacy have no idea of the responsibilities that come along with the title. These young men are the product of having proper guidance through spiritual fathers and mentors who have taught them the word of God. These young men have an array but no discipline or enlightenment of the price paid to build the Churches they are preaching in. The Church suffers greatly at the hands of young preachers with no values. Moreover, these young are being voted into Churches because there are not qualified candidates due previous generation lack of quality sons to replace them. According to Matthew 17:17, the bible says, "Then Jesus answered and said, O faithless and perverse generation, how long shall I be with you? How long shall I suffer you? Bring him hither to me.

Man has stepped in the pathway of Church history and has stepped over boundaries that were not meant to be compromised. The heart of the matter is humanism has stepped in and mixed information about the apostle and merged it with regard to the bishop to the point of confusion. How does an appointed position supersede and function called and petitioned from heaven. Unlike the bishop, the Apostle does not have a regional limitation. Some are called to regions, the nations and the Church in a particular sphere. The bishop has a different scope of influence to an area where a need must be acknowledged and where there is no other bishop in that particular region. Just like corporate America has some in the sphere of finances and some have a sphere in management. Both of them provide managerial expertise but at different levels of management.

Some historians have twisted their understanding of the anointing to shepherd and one called to the function as a shepherd. This pattern of thinking has taken root in every conceivable function, office and position. Unfortunately, this undaunted pattern has done more damage than good because too many confuse the seasonal anointing with that of the function. Unfortunately, this pattern has been entrenched in our society with those who have the audacity to question the historians by asking a simple question. Theology and philosophy has been a major vehicle in the posture of religion and purported in Christianity. Who said the pastor was in charge? Who said a person could function in multiple callings? Who said that anyone can take a position only because he or she desired it? What does the bible say about this? Why don't we see this being implemented in the Church? Who authorized an appointed position of Bishop to take over the authority of an affirmed function of an Apostle? Who said that an Archbishop and Apostle are one and the same? Where do we get these inconceivable notions? God authorized Jesus Christ to be the giver of gifts and to assume the role of each gift from the highest to the least. Self-affirmation and misuse of scripture in light of desiring the office is of the devil.

The body of Christ is experiencing many men and women who are counterfeits who take a position that is not conveyed properly. Needless to say, the philosophers and theologians have attempted to take something from the authority that can only be given by God and taken away by God as well. In other words, from a philosophical and theological perspective, apostolic succession does not follow the principle of a seed being reproduced after its own kind. However, the mere attempt to foster counterfeit is a unique attempt to violate scripture in context for the sake of validating the erroneous authority of the bishop. While the apostle can flow in other gifting(anointing), let us not assume that they walk in all functions. Doing it is purely a violation of scripture and the human attempt validate an office that was only assigned to do administration for the work established by the Apostles. The mere gesture that anyone called into office of the Apostle could grant another person the calling in which they have is in its own right scriptural negligence.

This is a clear indication of spirit of error being passed on as the truth. Truth and present truth shall always prevail even in the midst of those remnants of the Lord. Can we assume that the bishop has delegated responsibilities and can never transfer the authority granted by God to a position that is an appointment. Timothy and Titus were recorded as the only other bishops besides Christ who also had the calling of the apostle. The mystery behind the office of the bishop was not to take over the role of apostles as some seem to think and imagine. The function of the apostle did not die way, it simply went beyond the veil to return in the appropriate time. Death of the function would have meant that it could never return. The premise here is the mandate to embrace of the function of the Apostle. In other words, the apostle would have to return in order to start the New Testament Church and it surely needs to be in position for the return of Christ. The bible says in

Matthew 20:16, "So the last shall be first, and the first last; for many are called, but few are chosen. This scripture basically deals with being a servant of God and not necessarily geared towards a secular or spiritual position the Church.

Chapter 11:

The Expose of Gift, Character & Accountability

As we delve deeper into the history of the modern Church, we have uncovered a serious abatement from normality of a simple but strong foundation of order. The tendency to cover up the vile things indicates Church leaders need serious assistance. Occasionally, the cover up involves notorious acts conveyed by children of esteemed leaders. The fathers do not desire to be exposed, although exposure would allow the world to see their children have normal struggles just like the rest of the world. Yet, they would rather keep this hidden from those outside the Church. This indicates more leaders have surrounded themselves by an invisible veil to conceal them from being exposed. The concealment has perpetuated a cloak for the privileged to deny the command to walk uprightly. However, within concealment, there is more work to cover up a fault or sin than to come clean and reveal the truth.

This places us in the paradigm shift to prevent crop failure from becoming a reality. The Church is likened to a seed that has a tremendous disparity in regard to seeds cultivated by older preachers and seeds cultivated by the new breed of young preachers. The crop of young preachers make no fault in their desire to displace older preachers in lieu of the fame derived from large platforms and new dimension of notoriety. A strong displacement of loyalty exists with the young preachers who are inpatient at waiting for their opportunity to have the reigns of the Church. The vicissitudes of the young protégés carry a strong burden to seemingly feel that it is their time to take over and take charge of the Church. The burst of vigor and vitality of this new breed of preachers is armed and dangerous. The undaunted ability to preach and teach the unadulterated word of God has been overshadowed by the fact that integrity and character have been abated. In other words, the young preachers have a tendency to leave the pulpit to land in the bed of their choice of mate for a casual affair. Both young and older preachers lack certain intangibles of righteousness that should be a standard of living for all men who profess Jesus Christ as their savior. It is very condescending to see these men and women preach the gospel but have a tendency to live contrary to the word of God. The bible says in I Corinthians 9:14, " Even so has the Lord ordained that they which preach the gospel should live of the gospel."

A counterfeit or a hypocrite is a better indicator of one who professes to live righteous in front of the Church parishioners but is ashamed of the gospel around non believers. These leaders should be a true examples in front of everyone. The spirit of religion has cultivated a mindset that allows the manifestation or the imitation that produces an output that mocks the true life of a righteous person. The lifestyle patterns between the young and older preachers are drastically different. The older preacher has the tendency to be more like the turtle and the younger preacher acts just like the hare. The parallel between two is so profoundly similar that looking through the eyes of binoculars you would think they are one and the same. The simplistic steps of the turtle would give you a similar pattern for the older and much wiser preacher. While the older preacher walks in assurance of the simple things characterized by the grace of wisdom, the young preacher carries the vigor of the hare with an energetic burst to take off by pure ability and excitement with no practical level of wisdom. The un-settling notion held by these young preachers is an increased desire to replace their predecessor and activate their new and progressive agenda.

It apparent these younger preachers are eager to launch their new agenda which will truly place the Church under a massive burden of debt by trying to expand the Church with either a new fellowship hall or new Church building. The young preacher's actions are totally based on their opinion and the egotistical emotion. This new found ego precipitates a system that desires to abdicate totally from any sense of accountability. Some of these young preaching protégés have unleashed a frightening trend, to expand the kingdom by pushing out the older preachers to be crowned the new prince of the Church. This new direction could potentially be extremely dangerous to the body of Christ and its kingdom mission.

While these eager beavers desire to be positioned in the authority seat, they lack the sensitivity of the plight and struggle of the seasoned preachers who endured the tremendous strides to pay off the mortgage and burn the deed. Placing immature people into mature leadership roles prematurely stifles the entire body of Christ to the point of shipwreck. Age, giftedness, ability and charisma should not be automatic qualifying factors in determining if one is mature enough for ministry function. Character development is acquired over time and should be a driving factor in determining if one is ready to lead or not. Longevity, on the other hand, should be looked at from a different set of circumstances. While it is appreciated that some may have a decent track record of tenure, it does not necessarily mean that they have mature progressively during their journey. It is true that a protégé can be around you for years and still exhibit child-like tendencies that indicate they are not ready to lead anyone. As mentors and spiritual parents, we must re-examine from a biblical perspective in close examination of what the scriptural basis for elevation. These young protégées don't have the tenacity or the insight to start Churches from the beginning. They have an ability to preach but no insight for formulating and establishing a Church from ground up. The problem with this generation of preachers is they are visionless to the point that they would rather take over a Church than start one from scratch. This transition will direct and propel the Church into misery. This fearless mindset places the burden on the backs of the Church members, often times with dwindling membership due to retirement or teens going off to college.

The lack of accountability places the Church in the wayward hands of a gifted preacher with no precedence for traditional values. The essence here is the young preacher may have an enormous ability to preach the unadulterated word, but lacks the seasoning traits that would give him the business acumen to keep the Church out of harm and danger. These protégés exhibit such a desire to be in the position of great influence that the older Church members fear that he or she will leave at the first encounter of the opportunity for a Church with a large congregation and the ability to pay a much larger salary, the protégé will depart. Thus, money, prestige and respect of peers is more desirable to the young preachers than giving more allegiance to their creator. Although it appears that these young protégés care, because they need the people to carry out the vision. It is clear that the appearance is greater than reality.

The fruitless value system of the young preachers seem to be unsettling because their seems to be a lack of respect for people who have paved the way for these young preachers to rise out of flames of obscurity. It is safe to say this new breed of preacher does not have the complete package to run the Church in an effective and efficient manner. Maturity is required to gain all wholesome ingredients for effective leaders and leadership. Most of these first time neophyte preachers need to keep and maintain mentors and some level of accountability in order to be successful in this position. The position of Pastor does not only require you to preach and teach but also requires offices hours for the purpose of business affairs, counseling and meeting the needs of the flock. In addition, the plight of placing these young preachers in the position is doing more harm than good. Although many of these young preachers are rising at an alarming rate, the missing ingredient of the intangibles that seem to be the key elements for which this chapter emphasized.   The Bible says in Proverb 14:12 "There is a way that seemeth right unto man but the end thereof are the ways of death." The writer in proverbs epitomizes an indication that there would be a time where a great misfortune has taken affect. This pattern of thinking causes more concern and caution because they have either paid off their mortgage or they are very close to burning their deed. This disarray can be defused when the young neophytes can get their heads out of the air of obscurity and come down to reality. Part of the problem is that these neophyte preachers demand respect, but they have not been proven as effective leaders.

Furthermore, the inconsistent behaviors and the lack of experience will cause most of these neophytes to have a nervous break-down. Because of the thorough bread mentality, these young neophytes feel that they are invincible & indestructible. It is almost superficial to think that these young neophytes clearly do not comprehend the need to be well rounded in faith, business and their lifestyle. Moreover, the life style of these young minds need to be balanced as oppose to being extremely wayward in the pattern or disposition. The veracity of mindsets between the young and older preachers are at an impasse where the spirit of collaboration does not exist. The problem is that each one need each other but do not realize it. A rite of passage takes place when the timing is right for the older preacher to pass the torch to the younger preacher. The Church continues to operate on edge because they never know what to expect with these young radical preachers. In times such as these, there is an old adage that the bigger the Church the better. Needless to say, this mindset continues to foster more than the Church can endure. In given situations, character issues are prevalent with more young preachers who have a country club mentality rather than a standard of holiness. Furthermore, the younger mindset is more acclimated to the world system of filling up the Church with new membership but lowering the bar of holiness.

This mentality of allows a new age mindset to materialize inside the Church which is bewildering. This sudden trend epitomizes the great fall away from corporate worship to entertainment. Instead of evangelism in the purest sense of the word, there is a movement where people would rather go after neighboring Churches members in order to recycle believers from another Church than to go after the un-Churched.   This is a lazy approach and it breeds a celebrity mentality. This pattern of thinking prompts one to ponder, is it safe to invite this particular preacher over for fear of him stealing the sheep. How can fellowship take place where trust does not exist? The mega Church movement has become detrimental as more people insinuate that success for a preacher is defined by the number people being led. This new age thought indicates that a small crack gives access to the Church that promotes a missive for success based off numbers. Because our society believes that numbers don't lie, the tendency to measure a preacher's ability is determined by the size of the flock and the newest facility.

On the contrary, a Corporate Rader is one who takes over companies either to break the bigger companies into smaller ones or eliminates a company to add to a bigger pool of businesses. The Bible says in Acts 2:47, "Praising God, and having favour with all people. And the Lord added to the Church daily such as should be saved." The reference here is that God, in his infinite wisdom has added those who understood and obeyed righteousness and holiness to the Church. While man has tried to duplicate the authority of God in Kingdom business through a worldly business model to add to their empire, it will not be profitable because man does not carry the same authority that God carries.

Chapter 12:

The Malachi Mandate

The bible clearly speaks that the first shall be last and the last shall be first. In this case the last verse in the Old Testament Malachi 4:6 states, "And he shall turn the heart of the fathers to the children, and the heart of the children to their fathers, lest I come and smite the earth with curse." The significant details of turning the hearts of the fathers to their children has been adequately labeled "The Malachi Mandate." In this expression of the mandate, A fathers Heart being turned to his children means that he has a deep heart's desire to see each child grow up to be a man or a woman after Jesus heart. The father will make provision to assure that each child and grandchild will remain faithful to following Jesus Christ. From a spiritual standpoint, the spiritual father will make sure that each child shall be adequately prepared scripturally, mentally and physically. The scriptural basis for the father and son reconnection is best stated in Deuteronomy 32:46, "And he said unto them, set your hearts unto all the words which I testify among you this day, which ye shall command your children to observe to do, all the words of the this law." "For it is not a vain thing for you; because it is your life: and through this thing ye shall prolong your days in the land, whither ye go over Jordan to possess it."

The act of turning the hearts of the fathers to their children creates a need for the fathers to teach their children the commands which will ultimately prolong their life span. Although this chapter focuses on the father, it is essential to note that both parents are critical for son-ship to be effective. It should be noted here that son-ship is a term that includes both male and female. We must be mindful that the spiritual side is denoted as the male side and the fleshly side is noted as the female. Most parents feel the need to take care of their children when they are sick. However, parents need to also ensure their children's spiritual well being is taken care of as well. As a result when the heart is transitioned, the heart is clearly opened for a deposit from the Lord. In Proverbs 2:1-5, states," My son, if thou will receive my words, and hide my commandments with the; So that thou incline thine ear unto wisdom [and] apply thine ear unto understanding; Yea, if thou criest after knowledge, [and] liftest up they voice for understanding; If thou sleekest her as silver, and searchest for her as [for] hidden treasures; then shalt thou understand the fear of the Lord, and find the knowledge of God.

God informs us that the fear of the Lord and knowledge of God comes when the heart of the Sons is turned toward his father and when he listens to his father's instruction. Unfortunately, the present Church has attempted to teach the fear and the knowledge of the lord by going around the true spiritual father and training the sons in the Church without the Spiritual father. The outcome provides faulty alternatives or substitute routes of turning their hearts to peers who cannot possibly serve in the stead of a patristic blesser. The patristic blessing cannot be given by mentor or substitute father standing in the gap for the one who has been given the assignment. In light of the wonderful opportunity to understand the spiritual blessing, the Church has left its members open to becoming physical orphans and spiritual orphans. Thus, spiritual orphans grow up without affection, affirmation, comfort, or love causing them to become dysfunctional citizens. As a result, they decide to live a life in isolation. Therefore, the after affects of being a spiritual orphan can be detrimental to the plight of the spiritual pathway. The danger is that these spiritual orphans grow up not having what they never received. Spirits are transferrable and the same goes for patterns that have been precipitated by a need for change. The above mentioned pattern would prevent a father from being intimate, patient, gentle, and comforting and an affectionate father. Part of the transitioning of the heart transition for the fathers to the sons is centered around helping the fathers prioritize the importance of the spiritually training their sons and their grandsons. In addition, helping the fathers see the utmost importance through being the example of Christ in their children's life.

A father needs to embrace his responsibility to conduct the spiritual training of his children. Moreover, men tend to run from their responsibility instead of taking full responsibility of their actions. The Church must assume partial blame as many refuse to allow spiritual training. Some feel that there is no need for spiritual training and some are just spiritually deaf. Additionally, there are some who believe that peer leaders have over stepped their boundaries in trying to take the place of spiritual fathers. According to Proverbs 13:24, "He that spareth his rod hateth his son: but he that loveth him chasteneth him quickly. A father whose heart is turned toward his children will discipline them and inform them of their negative behavior prior enforcement of the discipline. He will not delay the penitence because he knows that a child does not like to have discipline waiting for him later. In order to turn a Sons heart to himself, a father needs to administer love and discipline when the sons needs it. Allowing the sons do whatever they want to do will turn them into rebellious hard core individuals looking for trouble to find them.

There are many hindrances that prevent the fathers heart from being turned towards the children can best be described in Psalm 49:6-8:The scripture says, "They that trust in their wealth, and boast themselves in the multitude of their riches; None of them can by any means redeem his brother, nor give to God a ransom for him; For the redemption of their soul is precious, and it ceaseth forever; The he should still live forever, and not see corruption; for he seeth that wise men die, likewise the fool and the brutish person perish, and leave their wealth to the others. Their inward thought is, that their houses shall continue forever, and their dwelling places to all generations; they call their lands after their own names; Nevertheless man being in honor abideth not: he is like the beasts that perish. This their way is their folly: Yet their posterity approved their sayings. Selah"

Fathers tend to put more focus on making money or career advancement rather than tend to the real priorities, the souls of their children. In the Father's heart transition to the sons, fathers need to see the foolishness of life in accumulating wealth in light of eternity. They need to see that the souls of their son is more important than owning land or houses. It is a certainty that the houses and land will not continue forever but the soul of the child will once they embrace the Kingdom of God. One of the common things that Sons has as an occurrence with fathers who tend to withdraw from their sons and daughters both spiritual and natural to pursue from their sons and daughter to pursue financial gain. The father must seriously refocus, refuel and reflect on the things are most important to the Kingdom of God. As we look in the Church, there is a vast difference between the father in the spirit and the father in the natural. The verity between the natural fathers is slightly different than a spiritual father. The spiritual father may have more influence but it is the same nature of the natural father because there is a divine connection. The key to adapting to your spiritual children is willingness to relate with the younger generation.

The spiritual application could place one in a position that your spiritual leader may or may not be older in the sense of chronology of age. Fathers have a tendency to make one to think that because of age, one cannot learn from someone from a younger generation. A typical notion of some spiritual fathers is one that he must be older than his spiritual son. This is a faulty notion that is based on the preponderance of age. God is the one who designates who is the son and who is the father. The physical aspect of fatherhood can be clearly identified by both mother and father. In addition to father assisting the wife in pregnancy, it is clear in the early stage of child rearing that it is done primarily by the mother. The mother, on the other hand, also helps develop the tender side of the sons. Sometimes life experience brings about better unique challenges that foster an opportunity to learn from one another. There will be many mistakes and misunderstandings between the father and sons as the father learns this important skill of relating with the younger generation.

The Spiritual leader needs to understand that he needs the support the entire family and exhibit traits of relating and leading the younger generation. Everyone has an opportunity to learn things because we all have something to bring to the table. In 1 Timothy 3:4-5: One that ruleth well his own house, having his children in subjection with all gravity; For if a man know not now to rule his own house, how shall he take care of the Church of God? A key to the being an effective spiritual leader (father) is to learn how to relate to his sons and that he first know their hearts. The sons need to know that their father truly loves them and is truly interested in their success in life. Family relations must be strengthened by the Church and their designated programs. The Church must be careful not to implement programs that draw the hearts of the sons from their father. The dysfunctional family structure plays a vital role in deterring the children's development. Some of the kids raise themselves with a father figure in the house. Many single mothers make poor decision and have several children by different fathers. Some men that do take care of their responsibility are forced to include the other siblings in their time spent with their kids. This creates a burden on the fathers to spend additional money on kids that are not his legal responsibility. However, in our society, there are good men who do take time out with the entire family in order not create a hostile environment for the child that is their legal responsibility. There are certain economic conditions that prevent some fathers from being in their children's lives. Some of the fathers have other children by other women and the task of uniting to children to meet their other brothers and sisters which creates a synergistic atmosphere of strong family ties. There are situations where good men marry women who have children and their families are blended. Each person plays a vital role in taking on additional responsibilities of children that have different parents whom are outside of the home. In matters such as, there is a potential for chaos when the father who has been missing in action tries to rekindle a relationship with the children abandoned. Good fathers will enable the children to reach out to their natural father to forgive and forget the past so that they can have a promising future. In summary, the intent of this book is to show the disparity in the Church and the present deformed posture of the Church and the posture that God depicted in His intent for Church.

A REFLECTION FROM THE AUTHOR

The author's intent is to show how the Church must realign its posture according to the true biblical blue print that God has given. This book is long over-due, but now it has come to fruition. It is the author's intent that every Church should be realigned to bring forth Gods manifested Glory to His Church. This book was not intended to malign all the pastors who step into the pulpit thinking they have been granted access but rather to look to God as to whom he gave the vision to and to adapt to visionary as the Senior Leader, who may not be a pastor per se. In other words, someone outside of the office or function of a pastor's realm may have been given the vision but he or she has been given the mandate to place the right people in the right positions. This does not negate the pastor's role in feeding the flock or having a part in the internal administration of the Church. Neither does it hinder the Church's flow when the right parts are allowed to take its proper place in the Church. The previous pattern of the position of a Pastor only Church had been a delusion in the historical precedence of the operation of a Church. There is a need for those who have identified their true calling to abandon the notion that they have to hold on to an office in which they were not called.

Rebellion has been a deterrent in the Church for change but now it is time to change for the Good of the God who has graced us with His mercy. How long do you continue to work with the wrong blue print? Because the Church continue to use the function of a Pastor only system, God has allowed a strong delusion to come forth which would enable new Church formations to continue doing the same pattern of things due to the pattern of feelings that have been conveyed. In other words, it is the feel good syndrome. This syndrome allows us to move by a feeling as oppose to moving by the spirit of God. The author has benefited from this writing which shall profoundly impact him in how he presides over his church, his fellowship and his life. This book has been such a pleasure and a blessing to write. Thank You Lord for giving me this book to write for the Kingdom of Heaven is at hand

ORDER ADDITIONAL COPIES TODAY!

BEHOLD THE HAND OF GOD, THE RIGHT HAND OF FELLOWSHIP IN A LEFT HANDEDED WORLD

Please send _____ copies of Behold the Hand of God, The Right Hand of Fellowship in a Left Handed World! By Archbishop K. Dewayne Grimble @ 14.95/copy, 1.20 taxes, 2.47 for shipping & handling. I have enclosed a money order, cashiers check payable to Kenneth D. Grimble for$_____

Mail to: P.O. Box 3001 Springfield, IL 62708

I can also order online @ http://k2kicc.info or http://archbishopgrimble.info

Name:_____

Address:_____

City:_____ State:_____

For More Information concerning the Kingdom Convergence Ministry of Archbishop Kenneth D. Grimble, feel free to visit our website.

http://archbishopgrimble.info

Feel free to write us at:

Archbishop Kenneth D. Grimble

P.O. Box 3001 Springfield, IL 62708

Email:Archbishopkdgrimble@gmail.com

www.ingramcontent.com/pod-product-compliance
Lightning Source LLC
LaVergne TN
LVHW021457080426
835509LV00018B/2317